Renaissance Humanism and Christopher Marlowe

A Study of His Plays

Renaissance Humanism and Christopher Marlowe

A Study of His Plays

R.K. Sharma
Ved Parkash Sharma

ATLANTIC
PUBLISHERS & DISTRIBUTORS (P) LTD

Published by
ATLANTIC
PUBLISHERS & DISTRIBUTORS (P) LTD
7/22, Ansari Road, Darya Ganj,
New Delhi-110002
Phones : +91-11-40775252, 23273880, 23275880, 23280451
Fax : +91-11-23285873
Web : www.atlanticbooks.com
E-mail : orders@atlanticbooks.com

Branch Office
5, Nallathambi Street, Wallajah Road,
Chennai-600002
Phones : +91-44-64611085, 32413319
E-mail : chennai@atlanticbooks.com

ISBN 978-81-269-1635-1

Printed in India at Nice Printing Press, A-33/3A, Site-IV, Industrial Area, Sahibabad, Ghaziabad, U.P.

FOREWORD

The publication of this book in India, and in these post-colonial times, is a matter of considerable surprise. Only an intrepid and deeply committed scholar will work on Christopher Marlowe at a time when our universities seem to be competing with each other to decolonize our minds simply by jettisoning the majority of such mainstream British authors from their English literature courses. This is especially the case with many of our premier universities in the metropolitan cities. A very large number of Ph.D. research projects in these universities are on Indian literature in English or in English translation. Indeed sometimes these projects are on works and authors not available in English at all, not even in translation. Why such work should not be done under the rubric of and in a department of Indian Literature or Comparative Indian Literature remains a mystery. It is as if a dissertation on a Sanskrit literary or philosophical text were to qualify for a Ph.D. in English literature merely because it was written in English. Perhaps under the pretext of decolonizing our minds, departments of English are bent upon colonizing other language and literature departments!

In comparison with the many bright, young and professionally savvy scholars of the academic metropolis who are diversifying into such new areas, academics in most of our peripheral universities may appear to be living in a time warp, still discussing Wordsworth as a poet of nature or debating whether Hardy was an optimist or a pessimist. But I think what is missing in such work in terms of up-to-date scholarship and information is often compensated for by a depth and sincerity of engagement with literature. This book on Marlowe and the Renaissance is a wonderful illustration of this.

The idea of the European Renaissance holds a perennial fascination for the Indian academic in general and for the teacher and students of English literature in particular. And if a poll were conducted to identify the one English writer who represents the quintessential Renaissance spirit, it is almost certain that the overwhelming majority of scholars would vote for Christopher Marlowe. Both his life and works continue to fascinate the reader more than four hundred years after his death: his life for his rise from a relatively humble origin to the position of the foremost dramatist of his time, his allegedly shocking and heterodox views on religion and other subjects, his secret and shady assignments and his untimely and violent end, and his works for the overreaching heroes, with "aspiring minds" and souls "still climbing after knowledge infinite". Two interrelated terms sum up this traditional and influential view of Marlowe as a Renaissance man and writer: humanism and heroic individualism. However, the contrary view, emphasizing Marlowe's medieval and Christian heritage has been no less influential, and the conflict between these two views is seen in its starkest form in relation to *Doctor Faustus*, which for some is a representation of the essentially "Faustian" Renaissance man and for others a medieval Morality play. The value of this book lies in its negotiation, with the help of thinkers like Paul Oskar Kristeller, Nicholai Berdyaev and Jacques Maritain, of a "middle path" between these opposite views about the Renaissance and about Marlowe. According to the authors, Marlowe rejected the proposition that "free thinking" or expansion of the self necessarily involves a "divorce from the centre of Being" since he saw that the crying need of the age was a "philosophy of integration", a synthesis of Renaissance knowledge and medieval theology.

This book substantiates this view of Marlowe's intellectual position with the help of detailed commentaries on *Tamburlaine, Doctor Faustus*, *The Jew of Malta* and *Edward the Second*. These should be of great interest and value not only to students and scholars of Marlowe and the Renaissance in general but also to those interested, specifically in one or more of these plays. It must be noted though that the book makes no mention of recent developments in the study of Marlowe and the Renaissance such as New Historicist and Feminist readings or the shift from the term “Renaissance” to “Early Modern”. No doubt the reason for this was the lack of access to books and journals. In any case, mere access to these and the consequent updating of scholarship would have been no substitute for the author’s independence of mind and depth and sincerity of engagement with issues that refuse to lose their relevance in the whirligig of critical fashions. The book is thus a remarkable example of both the challenges and possibilities of academic life in the majority of our universities.

Rajiva Verma
Former Head,
Department of English,
University of Delhi

Preface

It is not that, since so much has been written on the literature of the English Renaissance from Chaucer to the first half of the 17th century, any attempt on an individual author or a collective study of the period from a particular perspective is redundant. The truth is that any attempt, be it a study of an individual author or of a group sharing a common article of faith, like the playwrights popularly known as the University Wits, if it takes us ahead even by inches from the existing scholarship in the concerned area, the attempt is worthwhile, having a perennial literary value. Since writing, be it creative or critical, is an ongoing process, a tradition of much wider significance, we do not profess that the present modest attempt is a class performance, but without sounding presumptuous we do claim that it will certainly update Marlovian scholarship and enlighten the young researchers working in the area.

There is much controversy in regard to Marlowe's projection of the image of man in his plays. Some have admired his protagonists' attitude of defiance and protest against the eternal laws of nature and the world, others have condemned them for fostering the individualistic values. The 18th century rationalism, for example, did not appreciate much of the romantic exuberance and fancy pervading Marlowe's plays. They find the action of Faustus' selling soul to the devil "a mere barbarous survival from an age of superstition" and "if not offensive at all events absurd". But the romantics, when after the French Revolution even the slightest assault on human dignity was met with resentment, showed a regard for the expansion of self and had sympathy for the aspiring rebel. The Victorians continued to follow the lead as taken by the romantics. The romantic challenge to the 18th century common sense and reason created an intellectual stir in the early part of the 20th century and Marlowe's view of man in relation to self, society and universe began to be appreciated in right perspective. Harry Levin's tag, "overreacher" suggests the tragic irony of being human: there is an upward thrust in man as in nature to be what one is not, that has its own morality. There is nothing wrong in making a bid to surmount a fate to reach the unreachable because it is this which sustains the illusion of human reality. But what is essential is that the striving be not perverted by the notion of romantic liberation of self. It is the striving that involves the creation of a value, a desire to translate into action what one wills to attain.

Humanism, as its name implies, renders man "truly human" by way of freeing him from the medieval subjection and putting him on the path of self affirmation. But the whole venture verges on tragic irony: man could not escape the illusory notion of false humanism which brought his shift from the centre to the periphery. As such, the Christian concept of the universe began to lose its strength and the co-existence of the natural and the spiritual man was broken. The Renaissance humanism was not a sudden eruption, it was rather a gradual development and an awakening of the mind to enable man overcome what Blake called the "mind-forged manacles". The attackers of humanism exploit this proposition to mock at the humanist's claim that humanism has liberated man. What has it freed man from? They have in mind the anti-humanist flavour of anthropocentrism which, contrary to the orthodox theology, glorifies man to be his own centre in the scheme of things and generates in him the false notion of self-sufficiency to the extent of allowing God no intervention in human affairs. This is the self-destructive nature in humanism Berdyaev speaks of: once when man gets alienated from God, the rhythm of life is destroyed.

The theocentric concept of the universe—"that the centre for man is God" does not deny man the full use of his latent powers, as revealed by the discoveries, nor does the self-assertion cut off man from his vertical allegiance—dependence on God, "his spiritual limitations as a fallen being, and his spiritual potentialities as a redeemed creature." The truth is that it is the "divine direction" and illumination that saves man's social life from degenerating into the anarchic affirmation of self, verging on barbaric primitivism. The literature beginning from the Renaissance, which records the pride in the discovery of the universe and the man to the modern times, clashes at every turn with the humanist claim and the 20th century response—"things fall apart, the centre cannot hold" is the cry of despair but prophetic. The centre loosens its hold and things fall apart when man misunderstands his self in relation to time and begins to interpret the world as it looks to him, being unaware of the fact that "the world does move" and goes its own way beyond human comprehension. The Renaissance humanism is not a philosophical tendency in its origin but it influenced the philosophical thought of the time and provided many general ideas which were later developed into the definite philosophical theses and doctrines. The strength of Marlowe's humanism thus lies in the creation of higher consciousness and self awareness in relation to time: when the myth of the "fall of man" still continues to haunt human mind, how could the schism with the past satisfy the cravings of human spirit? A look into the literature of the past shows a parallel run of the false variety of humanism to true humanism but the proposition of "decentring the centre" did not wholly appeal to human mind and thus triumphed the spirit of true humanism. What was of particular interest was to separate the chaff from the grain. The exponents of anthropocentric humanism were in the dark about the moral hazards involved in seeking a wilful divorce from God. Such a world outlook drove them, not towards self-realisation, but alienation and spiritual enfeeblement.

Ever since the revival of the classical antiquity in Italy, attempts have been made at reconciling the two forms of humanism. M.M. Mahood has rightly pointed out that we find a theocentrically humanist spirit pervading the thirteenth century art of Italy, "the age of St. Francis, Dante, Giotto" and if later Italy "fostered the most violent travesties of humanism", there also "runs through the Italian Renaissance as well as that of France and England a vein of purest theocentric humanism." It is this paradox of literature of belief and unbelief that makes the Renaissance literature interesting. A forward step in the shift of the development phase of human understanding and wit makes man aware of the significance of the dialectic of "change and continuity"—"change" implies departure from tradition and "continuity" is "a connected whole" which in simple sense means the inclusion of what goes before and after.

The evolution of new humanism as M.M. Mahood maintains, issues from the integration of the theocentric and the anthropocentric world outlook which is achieved through the "continuity in change" that involves no disruptive break with the medieval thought and which finds full endorsement in Marlowe. The Renaissance was "disaster" in the sense that its benefits made human imagination run riot to the effect that man being drugged by hysteria of self-sufficiency "cut himself adrift from his supratemporal origins." The result was the moral decadence of which Marlowe was fully aware and sought in his plays the true spirit of humanism for man to realize, as the self-annointed godhead Tamburlaine of the play does at the end in Part-II—"Shall sickness prove me now to be man?"—that he cannot be more than human. The utterance is certainly human utterance. Hence the world outlook of Marlowe's heroes, as shaped by the spirit of anthropocentrism is, in fact, a form of theocentrism. The dilemma of this "continuity in change" is central to Marlowe's espousal of the philosophy of integration between tradition and modernity, and between true and false form of humanism.

The classical notion of humanism is characterized by "scholarship" and "learning", that of the modern by emphasis on "moral values" and "human welfare". If examined in the framework of this definition, Marlowe is a humanist but whether his humanism is theistic or atheistic is not a point of debate because neither view is wholly right or wrong to resolve man's dilemma in regard to reality which Marlowe presents in his plays. Both, when stretched to extremity, cease to mean anything distinctive. The medieval theology held that man is because he believes, to it the Renaissance answer was that man is because he thinks and acts and discovers. But does discovery imply holding one's supremacy over the other? Or do "free thinking" or expansion of self which in humanism are the core virtues mean seeking wilful divorce from the centre of Being? Marlowe rejects such a proposition and recommends the "middle path" with the conviction that, "one can be pro-man without being anti-God" which is at the centre of the humanism of the Greeks known as Christian humanism, as was revived by the bishops in the Middle Ages.

The "middle path" implies the avoidance of religious extremism or doctrinaire beliefs, it is the "golden mean" that keeps man's spiritual constructedness unimpaired and satisfy, at the same time, the urge to measure his strength against nature. A widespread preference for blind faith is not to be preferred to "no faith" that takes man away from the moral truths as enshrined in Christianity. The believer, knowing that there is some wrong somewhere which needs to be reexamined and reorchestrated in human context, evolves his dialectic of faith, the quest of which leads to the diffusion of issues pertaining to epistemology and illumines the dark in human mind. Man, as free man, may reject dogma or the superfluous rituals which lie beyond the computation of human reason but in the absence of the absolutes and the resultant religious uncertainties it is not worthwhile to be sceptic about the old unless the new, they seek to ideolize, fully fits into the moral scale of the humanist programme.

Marlowe's humanism is thus Christian humanism which is reflected in his emphasis on moral sense and in the extensive use of the pagan and the Christian resources in the interpretation of man and his environment. His plays show the fall of man—man left orphaned and defrauded by his worship of sham gods—who, in a bid to be more than human, ends as less than human (Faustus' wish to be born a brute is one fine illustration). In his theatrical universe those who disown their spiritual heritage and dream of becoming godhead are driven to despair and death. And, therefore, the crying need which Marlowe suggests for the age, by implications, is the philosophy of integration which can be achieved through the synthesis of the Renaissance knowledge and medieval theology so as to keep the equilibrium unbroken. The book will be useful for the students and teachers of English literature and researchers in this field, particularly Marlowe and his works.

Dr. Virender K. Roy who initiated us into interpreting Marlowe's plays from the standpoint of the philosophy of Renaissance humanism, read the entire manuscript with keen interest and the notes he put on the margin were rewarding in the pursuit of the line of query. To him we are greatly indebted. We also wish to thank the former Prof. B.K. Kalia of Kurukshetra University for procuring from his own library the material relevant to the area of study and the authors, like Jacob Burckhardt and Paul Oscar Kristeller—"a prime authority on Renaissance humanism and philosophy" who are today hardly seen on the university library selves, or are out of print. He also saw during discussions that the claim and values associated with the Renaissance, "a critical transitional period between medieval and modern ways of thinking" are illustrated and exemplified in terms of perspective in the study. The discussions were of immense value, centering around certain areas, like Marlowe's use of classical learning in the interpretation of contemporary reality and tracing the links between the intellectual history and thought of Renaissance and ancient sources. Prof. Rajiva Verma, Former Head, Department of English, University of Delhi has been very generous to write an insightful Foreword for the book. We are beholden to him. We are also thankful to Atlantic Publishers & Distributors (P) Ltd. for evincing interest in the publication of the book.

Rewari

R.K. Sharma
Ved Parkash Sharma

Contents

1

Introduction

Setting the limits

Since the present study purports to examine Marlowe's plays in the context of the philosophical premises of the Renaissance humanism, it is peremptory to take a view of Marlowe's world outlook, how he stands in relation to time and the form of false humanism as espoused by his protagonists in a bid to be more than human which verged on tragic irony as a result of their failure to reconcile between the achievements and discoveries of the time and the central doctrine of the medieval theology.

Ever since his rise in the theatre, Marlowe became a subject of public enquiry and thus the routine questions shot at, such as—is he a radical or a conservative?—make the study of his plays all the more captivating in an age which was highly paradoxical: an age which, on the one hand, illumined what was dark in human mind and, on the other, continued to encourage belief in medieval obscurantism, superstitions, faith-cure, alchemy, moral backwardness, ghosts and witches who were literally burnt "along with persons suspected of heresy, of sodomy and other dangerous thoughts or particular actions".[1] The socio-historical context be also kept in view while passing judgement on an author's philosophy of life and art, as is reflected in his writings. In the words of Fredrick S. Boas

> The times were critical with the Queen's government constantly faced by perils both at home and abroad. It was dangerous for any man to step outside the bounds of the Elizabethan via media in Church and State.[2]

There were rumours and suspicion in certain quarters about Marlowe that he was intending "to join the Roman Catholic recusants abroad"[3] which shows that Marlowe's problem was not to choose between Catholicism and Protestantism, but to interpret Christianity as he understood it. There was a search for belief in human context. And therefore, it is not unnatural if at the level of intellect and philosophy the viewpoint of such a seeker after truth clashes with the existing order. Behind "his exposure of the weaknesses of Christianity and Islam we seem to come closer than before to his own creed. And what is more fundamental in Marlowe than any religious, or irreligious belief, his passion for beauty embodied in classical legend and myth irradiates, as has been seen, with flashes of dazzling splendour even the most murky and ensanguined episodes of Part II of *Taburlaine the Great*".[4] The performance was misconstrued in the sense that Tamburlaine's attitude to God and religion brought a charge that the dramatist was a revolutionary and an Atheist.[5] Later, other charges, like that he was a Machiavel and an Epicurean were also flung at him. And strangely enough, among the accusers there were his fellow dramatists, like Robert Greene and Thomas Kyd.

In Marlowe-criticism, the discussion of what goes as Marlovian Trinity—Atheism, Epicureanism, Machiavellianism —is rather inescapable. But in the present project these terms are given as much space for discussion as is necessary for the reason that they do not come within the scope of the study and moreover these terms today do not mean what they meant in Marlowe's time. It was the age of 'free thinking' but human mind was not fully emancipated from the medieval scholasticism and thus 'free thinking' was looked upon as something scandalous and incurred the charge of atheism. Boas observes how the term "Atheism had in the sixteenth century much of the sweeping sinister associations that 'Bolshevism' has in the twentieth century. It was a useful slogan with which to denounce doctrines of actions that challenged the constitutional ecclesiastical or secular authority".[6] However, since atheism, broadly speaking, reflects a verdict about God, in the context of Marlowe, it means the rejection of God. The

Random House Dictionary defines 'atheism' as 'the doctrine or belief that there is no God or gods' but it also defines it as 'wickedness or immorality' which delimits its implication wholly to religion and thus the term itself becomes polemical. Critics have underlined passages of opposing shades in his plays: if they show the dramatist's hostility to all forms of institutional religion and revolt from, orthodoxy which on its negative side "went far beyond an assault on Biblical literalism and denial of the Incarnation,"[7] there are passages,[8] Boas quotes one from *Faustus* (Act I, sc-iii, lines 79-82), wherein Mephistophilis impresses upon Faustus how man's fall from God's grace implies damnation. Such a view, the critic says, shows that "the atheist Marlowe's conception of heaven and hell is more spiritual than that of the Puritan Milton in *Paradise Lost*".[9] Moreover, Boas takes a view that Marlowe's 'atheism' was largely shaped by the vision of the classical world opened to him through Rome and not through Greece, through Virgil and Ovid, no! through Homer, yet by nature he was less "an antique Roman than a Greek"

> But of Marlowe himself it may be said that during his lifetime his 'ghost' or spirit kept company with the old philosophers, including among them the myth-makers of the ancient world, and that what his contemporaries called his atheism was largely a legacy from them.[10]

Marlowe's humanism is reflected in his attitude to the divine which has human implication, not metaphysical or supernaturalistic. In this regard, Boas's observation is pertinent. "Divinity was primarily revealed to Marlowe in neither its Old, nor its New Testament manifestations, as the All-Righteous or the All-loving but under its Hellenic aspects of ideal beauty and 'knowledge infinite."[11] And thus if Marlowe in the age of the rise of modern scepticism and a free, scientific spirit of enquiry into the nature of things, denied divinity to Christ and was branded as 'atheist', what of Unitarianism today that denies the threefold nature of God, and holds that Jesus was a man and therefore not divine and that "Christianity is not a series of creeds or definitions, but a way of life?" Thus, religion as a deeply-felt psychological experience becomes rationalistic in Unitarianism and tends to give way to a general humanitarian outlook. Hence, in the context of it, Marlowe's atheism is recognised as a "point of view which can be broadly designated as natural religion".[12] In the wake of the rising waves of Reformation and the resultant 'Division in Religion', when the intellectuals began to look beyond the orbit of Christianity itself, Marlowe is reported to have said: "That the first beginning of Religion was only to keep men in awe" which is the echo of "the pagan rationalism of Lucretius". But ironically the view was exploited by one, Richard Baines in his Note (published in 1594), denouncing Marlowe's opinion on religion. However, Marlowe's biographers find Baines' Note confused and disorderly for the reason that the original document is 'undated' and it does not show personal intimacy between the two. The accusations, therefore, are such "as might be made by anyone in London Bohemian circles and collecting the gossip current there".[13]

The (sincerity?) of Baines' incriminatory Note can well be judged, when compared with the accusations of his fellow dramatists. Robert Greene is one who in a pamphlet, *Groatsworth of Wit* (1592) reproves Marlowe for Atheism,[14] as having said 'there is no God'. Thomas Kyd is another, the chief rival of Marlowe as a tragic dramatist whose own conduct was under investigation for free thinking and libel against the state. Kyd called Marlowe 'irreligious, intemperate and of a cruel heart' and accused him of jesting "at the divine scriptures, gibe at prayer and strive in argument to frustrate and confute what hath been spoken or writ by prophets and such holy men". Many commentators see in Marlowe's death a manifest sign of God's judgement. Thomas Beard, the Puritan, is one such critic to see Marlowe's death as a punishment for 'atheism and impiety'.[15] David Bevington and Eric Rasmussen say that the testimonials showing Marlowe as an atheist "need to be discounted for their exaggeration and for their having been produced under legal circumstances we would regard as a witch-hunt". But they do not deny the reality that Marlowe "explored and even revelled in the intellectual scepticism, articulated by the mathematician and astronomer Thomas

Harriott, by Giordano Bruno (who visited England in 1583-85), and by other whom the age generally regarded as free-thinkers and 'atheists'".[16]

There was a general charge that Marlowe was a propagandist of atheistic views but at the same time the commentators have felt that one cannot be certain about the degree to which one is a non-conformist and a rebel against the authority. It is otherwise not possible to say what precisely was dropped from his mouth which was condemned as heresy. Boas does not find anything coarse or obscene in his writings which is attributed to him by his informers. To quote his words, their allegations "may have been vulgarized and poisoned version of Marlowe's denial of the divinity of Christ".[17] And the whole thing is otherwise subjectivistic because sometimes it so happens that the accusations tell more about the degree of understanding of atheism of the accusers rather than that of the author's himself.

The second heresy of Marlovian Trinity is Epicureanism[18] which is, accordingly to Harry Levin, *libido sentiendi*, 'the appetite for sensation', which the Christian orthodoxy denounced. The orthodox Christianity preaches contempt for a fondness for the good thing of life, "the lust of the flesh, the lust of the eye and the pride of life". These temptations are considered obstacles to the attainment of sainthood. What then remained for man to do was to continue to live with the trust in Providence or to rely on one's free will? The third heresy is attributed to the Italian statesman, Nicolo Machiavelli[19] (1469-1527). The advice, as put forth to the princes in the controversial book *The Prince* was viewed in terms of the individual whereas Machiavellianism is not characterized by individualism, rather it condemns individualism as "a mark of Satanism" the evils of which become glaring in the Elizabethan and the Jacobean drama. The Machiavellian percepts were much distorted and exploited to the extent that they began to be associated with something treacherous, opportunism, scheming and dissembling and the term Machiavelli became 'Machiavel', the epithet tucked at his name became a term of contempt.

Thus, if we take into account the implication of the three terms as Harry Levin writes—Epicureanism, 'the appetite for sensation', Machiavellanism, 'the will to power' and Atheism 'zeal for knowledge'—which have their own morality in the context of the philosophy of 'this worldliness' then the heretic about them seems to disappear. These terms like any other terms of philosophical jargon are both constructive and deconstructive. If they are looked upon as heresies for the reason that they defy the taboos of medieval orthodoxy they are, on the contrary, the leading motives of the humanistic drama the reality of which can hardly be overlooked. In the affirmative sense, these mysterious urges are the strongest drives that sustain in the existential sense the illusion of 'human reality'.

The 'term' defined: the classical and modern notion of humanism

The two terms 'Renaissance' and 'humanism' are controversial. The literary historians have had as wide opinions in regard to significance and characteristics of the Renaissance, the precise time of its beginning and ending, its relation with the preceding period and following it, and the quality of literature written during the period which is, in parts, medievalistic in its conception. One view, Paul Oskar Kristeller states, is that the Renaissance seems "to have lasted as much as four hundred years, or only 27 years, not counting the view of those scholars who think that Renaissance did not exist at all".[20] Numerous attempts have been made to define Renaissance but they are found inconclusive. Kristeller identifies the Renaissance with the historical period that extends roughly from 1300 to 1600. Jacob Burckhardt formulated the traditional view of Renaissance 100 years ago, the focus being on Italy in the fifteenth and early sixteenth century. "He described the achievement of the period in the arts, literature and scholarship and stressed such general characteristics as individualism, the revival of antiquity and the discovery of the world and man." Burckhardt is of the view that many characteristic features of Renaissance civilization appeared much later than in Italy in other European countries as a direct result of the Italian influence which is seen in visual arts and the Renaissance humanism, though the view is challenged by the French historians who stress "the independent contribution during and before the Renaissance of other countries". J.A. Symonds and others stressed the 'pagan tendencies' of the period while others stressed the thoroughly religious character of the Renaissance and the impact of the philosophy of reintegration between the Renaissance knowledge and the medieval fatalism which is more discernible in the religious poems of the 17th century poets. Still others analysed the Renaissance as "a broader European phenomenon, especially during the sixteenth century, and of exploring both the Italian influences and the national characteristics which the period assumed in each of the major European countries".[21]

The Renaissance, in the words of Lamartine, was man's discovery of self and the universe. According to the French literary historian, Hippolyte Taine, man, so long blinded, "had suddenly opened his eyes and had seen". The blindness is metaphorical, not literal, which can be better comprehended by taking into account man's geographical position narrowed down by the Mediterranean and the nations that clustered around it and the intellectual dictated by the power-seeking ecclesiastical authorities. The scholastic system of learning discouraged the free spirit of enquiry and all that could create doubt was condemned and suppressed. Man passively accepted what the church explained to him as the basis of truth. In spite of his eagerness to learn the laws of nature and the universe, man was kept aloof from the fruits of knowledge. The biblical myth of the fall of man was exploited by the church to warn man of the second fall, if he dared to indulge in free intellect. In other words, the craving for self realization, as revealed by knowledge, was condemned as something damnable. It was given to know that the Scriptures have all that man may come to seek to know and if there was something particular to interpret it was the job of the church and the schoolmen to do so, not of the common man. It is in this respect that the love of knowledge was looked upon as heresy and irreligious.

There is a misconception about the Renaissance being a sudden and violent overthrow of the medieval world order or that the reawakening of the human mind changed Europe overnight. Douglas Bush views the Renaissance as the development of an inevitable historical consciousness, occurring in stages—discovery, assimilation, expression and cites the cycle of cultural destruction and reconstruction in support of his contention: the Romans destroyed the Greece and were themselves in their decay overrun by the barbarians who assimilated the Greco-Roman culture which spread in its own way with no christian antagonism. The process gained momentum in the 12th and the 13th century and reached the climax in the 15th and the 16th century and was popularly known as the Renaissance. Gilson, perhaps keeping in mind much of evil and superstitions which continued to prosper in the Renaissance and dehumanized man, has gone to the extent of saying that "Renaissance was the Middle Ages minus God" which Paul Oskar Kristeller dismisses as 'unfriendly' and an exaggerated remark because the Renaissance thought, as the critic contends, was as a whole not opposed to or indifferent to God. He finds hardly any thinker who denied the existence of God.

The popular theory of the rise of this intellectual stirring in Europe is associated with the fall of Constantinople, a Christian state and the capital of the Eastern empire to the Turks in 1453. But if we look back at the contributions of the Italian scholars like Petrarch, Boccaccio, Luther, Erasmus, Thomas More and many more then it comes to revealing the truth that the fall of Constantinople is not the sole factor responsible for the rise of this new phenomenon in Europe. But it is true that after the fall of Constantinople, the Arab, Greek and Jewish scholars fled westward, carrying with them as many manuscripts as they could and sought refuge in Italy which not only gave them shelter but also accorded a welcome. Thus, there can be a dispute on the origin of Renaissance but no one can disagree with the view that Italy was the first country to be enriched by its flowering benefits.

Some scholars are of the view that this process of re-orientation of human mind began much earlier even before the Turks destroyed Constantinople and ransacked its monasteries. They hold that the awakening of European mind is the result of its interaction with the Arab mind in the twelfth century when during the Holy crusades the European soldiers met the Arabs, "not only in the battlefield but elsewhere too".[22] J.H. Plumb rightly observes that

> Europe of the Middle Ages was not a closed world. The Crusades had ripped open the Near East and given the hordes of warriors a taste of sophisticated, cultured society which previously had only been the experience of merchants and pilgrims. And Italy was the door through which the Crusaders passed.[23]

This contact created a zest for questioning the orthodoxy, man turned agnostic and began to take everything, not on the passive acceptance of the dogma but on what it came to be true by way of experience and experimentation. This is what it means by the rise of modern scepticism and the free spirit of enquiry in Renaissance which made man to "shake off the trammels of Roman authority and go forth and expatiate in the field of free enquiry".

And thus the rediscovery of the classics revolutionized man's world outlook, one implication of which was that under the influence of the spirit of humanism which opposed the philosophy of the schoolmen, 'scholasticism', the meanings of Christianity, as it was understood in the Middle Ages, ceased to appeal. Man shed the fear of purgatory. Jack P. Bernard's observation in regard to this secular philosophical shift is pertinent:

> Christianity, in the medieval understanding of that term had more or less ceased to have any meaning. Their heroes were no longer an Augustine, A Jerome, a Bonaventura, or an Aquinas, but rather Plato, Virgil and lesser denizens of the literary and intellectual pantheon of ancient Greece and Rome.[24]

The church which had a rich tradition of once being an intellectual and moral custodian of the masses loosened its hold, there were signs of decadence and enfeeblement when the clerical class felt drawn to the spell of capitalism. Gower attacks the church in his Prologue to *Confessio Amantis*, so does Chaucer in the Prologue to the *Canterbury Tales*, "If gold rust, what shall iron do" when he saw the lower segment of the society falling as much a victim of materialism as the bourgeoisie. As such, the belief in the spiritual discipline as a way to achieve redemption of soul from innate sinfulness ceased to fascinate him, he sought freedom from every bond—religious, political, social and moral. That is why the church was no longer a threat to his religious position, the king had no more control over his physical movements and the society composed of such free and independent individuals did not bind him in the chains of the ethico-moral codes. He did not look for salvation toward heaven because heaven and hell by themselves became a subject of sceptical enquiry.

What Berdyaev speaks of the self-destructive dialectic in humanism became the central reality, governing the philosophy of the Elizabethan world picture. Man by way of experience became aware of the natural energy and felt himself no longer a subject of moral scrutiny. H.B. Parkes brings out this dilemma of morality and value of the Renaissance man who found the void between the two hard to surmount.

> ...the Elizabethans were in a process of discovering by methods that man's natural energy was an amoral force which did not appear to conform with any traditional notions of goodness. On the one hand, they had been taught that nature was fundamentally good, that evil was a mere imperfection or aberration, and that the maintenance of moral and political order depended upon this belief in the identity of natural and divine law. On the other hand, they were confronted by a natural world in which the central reality was not reason or morality, but power, and the manifestations of power were, by traditional standards, evil. Evil, including all its destructive potentialities, thus appeared to be natural. They found themselves, therefore, torn between two

> kinds of knowledge with no way of bridging the gulf between them.[25]

Critics have demolished the wrong notion about Italy that in the Middle Ages it was as 'dark' from knowledge point of view as the rest of Europe was. J.H. Plumb writes,

> Throughout the Middle Ages the classics had been copied, studied frequently for their moral virtues, occasionally enjoyed for themselves. Monks appreciated Horace as well as Seneca, and even Ovid was not unknown to the cloister. There were high points of excitement and discovery. The recovery of many of Aristotle's works in the twelfth and early thirteenth centuries, from Arabic sources, created an intellectual ferment in scholastic circles.[26]

The historians of the Middle Ages also see no room for the 'rebirth' theory associated with the Renaissance. They have found the counterparts or precedents, peculiar to the Renaissance in the later phase of the Middle Ages. Thus, the period had its own achievement as a civilization and "was far from a 'dark age' that needed to make room for a period of 'rebirth'". Gordon Campbell is another to find the myth of medieval darkness rather ill-founded and incompatible with the spirit of the time.

> The notion of a medieval period of darkness and ignorance, stretching from the fall of Rome (or in the ecclesiastical model from the official adoption of Christianity as the state religion in the fourth century) to the sixteenth century will seem ridiculous to any one familiar with the accomplishments of medieval literature or to anyone who has visited the magnificent cathedrals of the period.[27]

The truth is that the Renaissance in Italy has a different story. Before the shift of learning from Constantinople to Italy took place, Italy, as the historians have shown, was familiar with the Greek literature but the same could not reach the rest of Europe for want of resources. It is thus not fair to underestimate the creative strength and originality of the fifteenth century Italy. The one aspect of the brilliance of

Renaissance Italy was art which "created an image of man, a vision of human excellence that still lies at the heart of the Western tradition". Second, the spread of knowledge, first being a localized phenomenon, was rather slow. And moreover, the ignorance and the superstitions associated with the word 'dark' cannot be separated from what is enlightenment and knowledge which persisted even after the advent of new learning. The two act as the structuralist binary oppositions like black/white, East/West, nature/culture which they hold that "such oppositions are basic to all cultural phenomenon, to everything from language to cooking". As 'black' has its meaning by 'white', so 'dark' derives its meaning from 'light' signifying illumination of human mind. There is in fact no dividing line between the two—one is abstract and dry without the other. Third, the threats of excommunications were feared more outside Italy than inside and as such the fear of attainment of knowledge died out which finds expression in the works of the period. In the words of M'Crie

> The Italians could not, indeed, be said at this period (fifteenth century) to have a superstitious devotion to the see of Rome.... The Republics of Italy in the Middle Ages gave many proofs of religious independence and singly braved the menaces and excommunications of the Vatican when all Europe trembled at the sound of its thunder.[28]

And otherwise also, in Italy there was no antagonism between the Renaissance and the Reformation as it was in England, the instant causes being material. The Reformation brought disunity in the church which meant the decentralization of the authority in the church-hierarchy for which Italy was not willing to have it so, as it meant a huge national loss in revenue that they collected from the other European countries for procuring investitures, books and other church articles for the bishops and the cardinals.

And second, the humanism kept the Italian writers aloof from being critical of the corruption in the church. Their pragmatic wisdom is manifest in the plea that "it is not wise to bite the hand that gives you bread". In other words, because the Popes and the cardinals were great patrons of art and learning, the masses had no antagonistic feelings towards them despite their suffering from moral laxity and irreligion. And moreover, the impact of such moral inadequacies were felt not so much in Italy as it was felt outside. Boccaccio's *Decameron* is a faithful record of all such excesses as the tales of Chaucer's pilgrims throw light on the diverse shades of the 14th century English society. There are numerous instances to show that Italy had the benefits of the spirit of Renaissance before Europe was inundated with Greek and Latin classics. One was the rise of a new philosophy under the impact of Plato which replaced the philosophy of the medieval schoolmen, known as 'scholasticism' and when combined with the humanist aspect of Christianity, not with its dogmatism, took a new name, neo-Platonism. It was accepted as the philosophy of Renaissance. Jack P. Bernard has summed up this assimilation of paganism and Christianity.

> After Petrarch the impact of this pagan culture was as powerful on the clergy as on the laity, but the foundations of Italian faith were not as much shaken as they had been by the heretical movements of the Middle Ages. The great majority of men who concerned themselves with humanities were equally expert in the divinities. Most of them held ecclesiastical offices, or belonged to the priesthood or the monastic or mendicant orders.[29]

The voice of Apollo, representing the religious and the philosophical spirit of the Greeks, was silenced when Christianity was declared as the state religion by emperor Constantine and became as the political force in addition to moral and spiritual in the fourth century but it is not something surprising it, in spite of the fact that Rome was the seat of the head of the Roman Church, the studies of the classics, as carried into Italy, were not banned. The simple reason was the awareness of the actual ideal of the Renaissance which was 'the universal man' or in modern sense 'a well rounded personality' which includes the harmonious development of all human endowments. The rivalry of the five dukedoms of Italy was a hindrance to effect the national unity but its one positive gain was that the Italian courts vied with each other on the issue of patronage of arts and learning.

Like the Renaissance, the term 'humanism' or 'Renaissance humanism' has come to mean many things to many people. With the rise of the modern notion of humanism, several schools of humanism have sprung up like theistic/atheistic humanism, scientific humanism, Christian humanism, existential humanism and the like which define the term altogether in a different way from what it was associated with in the Renaissance. Paul Oskar Kristeller says that it is the result of a tendency growing up today that if humanism is to be made acceptable to contemporary opinion it must be defined in terms of certain ideas and ideals which is perhaps due to "the declining respect for scholarship". Hence, there are issues which need our primary attention, like defining the term 'Renaissance humanism', its origin and place in the civilisation of Italy, its chronological limits and intellectual content, its nature and range of activities and its assimilation into Europe after its diffusion. The Italian scholars used 'humanism' for a period, namely the fifteenth century while others called the period of early Renaissance by the name of humanism which was the period of intellectual preparation, a period in which the Greek and Latin texts were introduced into the university curriculum and partly their translations were made to bring the wisdom of the ancients within the reach of the common man. Thus, humanism in the beginning meant an emphasis on classical scholarship and learning which characterizes the period. In modern notion of humanism, there is emphasis on human values and the thinkers, seeing its counterparts in Renaissance literature or in the literature of the past, have put on it a label like 'Renaissance humanism', 'Italian humanism' or 'Christian humanism' to the effect that the word 'humanism' has begun to mean an emphasis on human values which permeated in the Renaissance period. The humanism of the Renaissance was something different from the present-day interpretation. Every one interested in human values and human welfare would today like to be called a humanist in this sense of the word, whereas a 'humanist' in the Renaissance had a different meaning and the humanism of the Renaissance was some thing different from its present-day interpretation. It is true that the

> Renaissance humanists were also interested in human values, but this was incidental to their major concern, which was the study and imitation of classical, Greek and Latin literature. This classical humanism of the Italian Renaissance was primarily a cultural, literary, and educational movement, and although it had a definite impact upon Renaissance thought, its philosophical ideas can never be completely detached from its literary interests.[30]

Therefore, it is not unfair to say that humanism which contributed to the rise of Italian civilisation in the Middle Ages was called Italian humanism, likewise the contributions of the Renaissance thinkers who were influenced by the literary and scholarly flavour of the movement in the development of a vast area of learning and literature, we call Renaissance, is conveniently designated as Renaissance humanism.

Paul Oskar Kristeller says that what he understands by the term 'humanism' is that it is "a body of literature, scholarship and thought represented by the writings of the humanists" and the 'humanists' are "those scholars who by profession or vocation were concerned with the *studia humanitatis*". This leaves no room for misunderstanding and confusion if humanism is taken and examined in the context of the above what it came to mean later with its "vaguely conceived emphasis on human values that is supposed to be characteristics of the Renaissiance". And because the Renaissance humanism for its commitment to 'a cultural programme and ideal' has a distinct character of its own, it differs from

> ...vernacular literature, from technical philosophy as cultivated by the Aristotelians, the Platonists and the philosophers of nature, and from the university disciplines of mathematics, medicine, law, and theology. Humanism represented a body of scholarship and

> literature that was secular, without being scientific, and that occupied a place of its own, independent of, though not opposed to, both theology and the sciences.[31]

Humanism thus, as Paul Oskar Kristeller has stated, is secular, independent but not opposed to religion and science. But when the historians speak of Renaissance humanism, he continues, they speak of it in a different sense from its contemporary meaning. They are

> ...referring to a broad class of Renaissance intellectuals who are traditionally called humanists and who were active as teachers and secretaries, writers, scholars and thinkers; who exercised a wide and deep influence on all aspects of Renaissance civilization; and who left to posterity, along with the record of their lives and activities, vast writings that may be roughly classified as literature, historical and philosophical scholarship, and moral thought, but which often deal with such diverse subjects as philosophy and the sciences, literary and art criticism, education, government and religion. The revival of antiquity generally associated with the Renaissance period, the thoroughgoing classicism that we notice in all its literary and artistic manifestations, is surely the direct or indirect effect of Renaissance humanism.[32]

Konard Burdach owes the origin of humanism to religion and says that its secular orientation is a later development, Gueseppe Toffanin states that the rise of Renaissance humanism "was a Catholic reaction against certain heretical tendencies inherent in medieval thought", whereas Dogulas Bush sees in it a blend of reason and faith, he identifies the core of Renaissance humanism as "Christian humanism which shares with Thomas Acquinas the concern for harmony between ancient reason and Christian faith". To Eugenio Garin, humanism meant what "was best in the philosophical thought of Renaissance, stressing its preoccupation with the human and moral problems of the layman and its contrast with the theological orientation of medieval scholasticism".[33]

But to be more precise about the meaning of Renaissance humanism we have to go back to what the terms 'humanist' and 'humanities' stood for in Renaissance humanism. The term 'humanism' was associated with the classical movement of the Renaissance and was coined by a German educationist, F.J. Neithammer in 1808. It has another similar Latin word 'humanista' the English translation of which is 'humanist'.[34] The term 'humanista' which came in popular currency in the Renaissance period, comes from 'humanities'/'studia humanitatis'. The term was "apparently used in the general sense of a liberal or literary education by such ancient Roman authors as Cicero and Gellius and this use was resumed by the Italian scholars of the late 14th century".[35] A humanist was a professor or student of humanities which includes the study of the clearly defined scholarly subjects like grammar, rhetoric, poetry, history and moral philosophy. To this list was added the study of the Greek and Roman authors of classical antiquity. The Renaissance scholars turned to study and interpret the Greek and Latin classics for their concern and emphasis on human values, inherent in these subjects and on moral philosophy which is closely associated with the humanist movement. They are called humanists, as it is meant today, in the 20th century. Many among the humanists were the teachers of the humanities at the universities or in secondary schools and professional rhetoricians which included the secretaries to the princely courts and the cities, the writers and the critics. The teachers concentrated on the moral thought for the education of the young, their moral writings are replete with the quotations from the Greek and the Roman writers and episodes from classical history and mythology. The rhetoricians aimed at saying not only the truth but to say it well according to their literary taste and standard, laying emphasis on elegance rather than 'precision'. The Renaissance humanism is thus not as much a philosophy or a system of thought as it is a cultural and educational programme and in this sense, "must be understood as a characteristic phase in what may be called the rhetorical tradition in Western culture".

What are the channels through which was effected the diffusion of Italian humanism in Europe? Paul Oskar Kristeller counts three which are: (1) the exchange of persons of diverse degree and profession, including the merchants, the clergy, political envoys and the Italian students, (ii) their correspondences, and (iii) the manuscripts of the books and the printed editions which include the translations and imitations of the Italian humanists in the vernacular during the Renaissance. A single manuscript which was placed in a library and read by many was an important document for the intellectual orientation of the reader. Those who went to Italy on some business or on political trip made use of their stay to get themselves acquainted with the humanist learning but their cultivation of it depended largely on their period of stay and partly the area of interest. Some, as it is reported, went on their own to be familiar with the humanist programme and fashion their own view of man and the universe in their writings.

The students who visited Italy are also a substantial channel by which the humanist scholarship and learning made a passage to Europe. They stayed for several years in Italy, became familiar with the humanist programme and writings and on their return were offered places of importance in the government and the profession, thereby to serve an effective medium to make the programme popular. Besides, the Italian businessmen and the students were also an important factor to bring the humanist learning to Europe. There were Italian scholars[36] who entered into the service of the princes in Europe and their contact with the native scholarship was also instrumental in the spread of the humanist learning. Thus, as the account goes, a number of Italian scholars were assigned the job of teaching in the European universities which exercised a deep influence on the native genius. A last group of Italian scholars to come to Europe includes "the political and religious exiles".[37]

Much has been written on humanism from the standpoint of fitting it into the framework of theology, philosophy and history, each study has a print of bias which makes the task of finding a viable definition of the word rather arduous whether the term is a religious doctrine, a scientific theory or a term of ethics. The transcendence of subjectivity is hard to accomplish, Jacques Maritain's definition in *True Humanism*, in the accepted sense seems balanced.

> Let us say that humanism (and such a definition can itself be developed along very divergent lines) essentially ends to render man more truly human and to make his original greatness manifest by causing him to participate in all that can enrich him in nature and in history (by 'concentrating the world in man', as Scheler has almost said, and by 'dilating man to world'). It at once demands that man make use of all the potentialities he holds within him, his creative powers and the life of the reason, and labours to make the powers of the physical world the instruments of his freedom.[38]

The emphasis on 'participation' to enrich, not impoverish nature and 'original greatness' is significant which can be made possible by keeping the fact in view that there occurs no break between faith and unfaith and the equilibrium remains unbroken. The role of creative powers and reason does not exclude the role of the divine in the attainment of the humanist ideas and the original greatness by which Maritain means the greatness of the spirit be not smothered by man's own imperfect understanding of his place in relation to God and universe.

In the Renaissance, the study of the classics was, in simple sense, designated as 'humanism' one implication of which was of its having claimed to liberate man from the monkish superstitions of the medieval age and assure human freedom. But the concept was confounded with individualism which in the Renaissance context meant "the expression of individual subjective opinion, feeling and experiences". The stress was on the glorification of man and his dignity: man became sceptic of the divine machinery and began to look at the world on his own terms. This is how anthropocentrism made way which was condemned as atheism by the orthodox. There started a reaction against it in the Protestant circles condemning it as an irrational display of the depraved nature of man. The crucial question then was: whether man should continue to live with God or be his own God to live by in a universe that no longer looked stable to his eyes? For this epistemological and ontological puzzle, humanism is both attacked and defended. Some are critical of its illusory benefits but it is not the whole story. The fact that the age that fostered a Hamlet also fostered a Claudius is used as a testimony to suggest that each philosphy/system has some inherent good in its texts and it cannot be hostile to the humanist concern with the good of mankind as a whole unless it is put to disuse. Attempts have been made to separate the grain from the chaff. Maritain's distinction between the true and the false humanism—he puts it as theocentric humanism and anthropocentric humanism—is one such attempt to project its philosophical formulations in right perspective.

> The first kind of humanism recognizes that the centre for man is God; it implies the christian conception of man as at once a sinner and redeemed, and the christian conception of grace and freedom.... The second kind of humanism believes that man is his own centre, and therefore the centre of all things. It implies a naturalistic conception of man and of freedom.[39]

There are some who discover in the theocentric humanism something opposed to the humanist programme—man's dependence on God and thereby undermine human potentialities which is all a subjectivistic fallacy. The truth is that faith in providence does not deny man his humanity, nor does it discourage the free use of natural gifts which are God's endowments. Rather it is an obligation to seek their realization at the fullest. The growth of self-consciousness, as wrought by a radical change in man's world outlook in the age of discovery was abused to overstep human limitations which proved, overtly or covertly, a threat to the development of a truly humanist society. Thus, humanism proved the tragic flaw, in the Aristotelian sense, to bring the tragedy of man. The estrangement was self-anointed from within, not from outside. The attempt to restore equilibrium by way of falling back upon the exhausted resources brought no spiritual relief. The reason was the failure to reconcile between the modern and the medieval world order which assures the inner tranquillity that comes from an undivided mind.' Berdyaev sees in it the disintegrating symptoms of the humanist ideal.

> Humanism, as its name implies, denotes the elevation and setting up of man in the centre of the universe.... It has been said that humanism discovered the human individuality and gave it full play, freeing it from its mediaeval subjection and directing it upon free paths of self-affirmation and creation. But humanism also contained a diametrically opposite principle, that of man's abasement, of the exhaustion of his creative powers and of his general enfeeblement. For humanism, by regarding man as part of nature, transferred the centre of gravity of the human personality from the centre to the periphery. It divorced the natural from the spiritual man. It divorced him from the interior significance and the divine centre of life, from the deepest foundations of man's very nature; and it then gave him the freedom of creative development. In fact, humanism denied that man was the image and likeness of God; that he was the reflection of the Divine Being.... The Christian consciousness of man began to lose its strength. And this, in its turn, gave rise to a self-destructive dialectic within humanism.[40]

The humanism, as was nurtured by the liberal bishops in the Middle Ages, was Christian humanism of the Greeks, which was 'pro-man without being anti-God' the echo of which is manifest in modern Unitarianism, "to ignore God without repudiating him". Today a misconception about humanism pervades in many countries that 'living without God is humanism' which is a form of atheistic (anthropocentric humanism). Following this line Miriam Allen de Ford has gone to claim that "humanism must be atheistic or it is not humanism as I understand".[41] But our acceptance or rejection of this formulation depends on our understanding of what the critic meant by atheism because atheism by itself means differently to different people, there are some humanists who are atheists in that they view atheism as an intellectual doctrine that takes man away from the worship of the sham gods and puts him along the path of self-realization but 'all atheists are not humanists'.

Humanism is defended for its freeing man from the tyranny of the medieval world but it is also attacked for its forstering individualism and pushing man away from the centre, i.e. God to the margin, thereby falsifying the medieval concept of man being a creature of flesh and spirit "co-existed in two worlds". E.M.W. Tillyard sees man standing[42] "at the apex of Nature's pyramid with one foot upon the angelic order" and the view finds support in Thomas Browne's *Religio-Medici.*[43] And if man chooses otherwise the fault then lies not with the philosophy of humanism but with his own imperfect understanding of the theories and principles of humanism. Humanism does not consider man perfectable and the truth of it finds attestation in the failure of the humanists themselves to reach that 'standard' which they set forth to measure man. Man in all his complexities was a 'standard'[44] for the humanists. Jacob Burckhardt's two chief accusations are sufficient to show how they failed to attain the ideal which are "malicious self-conceit and abominable profligacy", a third charge of irreligion was now loudly added by the rising powers of the 'Counter-reformation' in the 16th century Italy. As such, "their doctrine and scholarship had lost hold on the public mind"[45] which brought a disgrace to the whole class of the humanists. The truth is that it is the true humanism which makes man aware of his moral inadequacies and impresses upon him the power of the spirit by which he, as 'a redeemed creature' can transcend those limitations. Those indulged in anti-humanist propaganda unleashed against humanism that it is illusory cite the literature of the Renaissance, particularly, the drama in support of their contention to mock at the wishful thinking of the Renaissance humanists who are happy at the conversion of Frederick and Oliver (*As You Like It*). But Shakespeare knows that in real life Fredericks or Olivers will never yield to the moral pressure of their victims. Hence, the need is to say something to see in what sense it is used today and how much its spirit is abused.

Let us look at the whole post-1453 scenario from the standpoint of the contemporary value-orientation. If the Renaissance is the discovery of man, it is also the discovery of the moral truths about man which is central in the philosophy of the theocentric humanism: that nature, when cut off from divine source, is not emancipated as the Renaissance man dreamt of but impoverished. In this sense, the Renaissance "appears neither calamitous nor sudden". If it was a disaster in the sense that it brought an upheaval in the traditional values it was so because the temptation to deny God became an overwhelming passion with man and the result was his alienation from the divine source of the being, as is rightly observed by M.M. Mahood.

> Human nature, thus estranged, is deprived of its main strength and flung upon its own quickly-exhausted resources: this is the self-destructive dialectic of which Berdyaev writes. Once the twofold rhythm of life in the middle state is destroyed, oscillations between unbalanced extremes ensue in every sphere of thought and action. Each new movement, each swing of the pendulum, seeks to restore the lost equilibrium, and each fails because of the self-destructive principle in humanism whereby 'when (man) lost the spiritual centre of Being he lost his own at the same time'.[46]

M.M. Mahood uses Ulrick von Hutten's cry "Spirits have awakened. It is good to be alive" to show the benefits of the rise of human consciousness which verged on tragic irony. There is nothing wrong with the cry but there is every wrong if the awakening sets human spirit upon what Berdyaev calls "a diametrically opposed principle in humanism". It also prompts another disturbing query; where then lies the tragic flaw-in man or in what the Renaissance associated with? The truth is that man's own inadequacies to surmount the time's disorders made a false variety of humanism triumphant which infected the social structure the process of which had begun earlier. Emile Brehiere calls it 'humanistic naturalism' which is akin to the Marxian concept of the role the sociological forces play in determining the ideas and ideologies of the time.

> ...the concept of theocentrism was gradually abandoned.: as early as the twelfth century humanistic naturalism emerged and focused attention on the study of the structure and forces of society; in the fourteenth century the Okhamists, deliberately neglecting everything that related to the origin or the end of things and even demonstrating the fallacy of believing that something of the divine plan could be apprehended in the contrast between the immutable heaven and the sublunary region, studied nature in and for itself. It was the next two centuries, however, that offered every reason for abandoning the concept of theocentrism.... The Christian drama with its historical moments-creation, sin, redemption-could no longer circumscribe a nature whose laws were completely indifferent to it, a humanity, one segment of which was totally ignorant of it, an era in which Christian themselves threw off the shackles of spiritual power and won acceptance in their politics of goals totally alien to the spiritual supernatural ends of the Christian life or even deliberately opposed to the idea of Chiristian unity.[47]

But it is not that the abandonment of the theocentric concept of the universe left man in a state of nowhereness or in darkness if looked at it metaphorically. The idea to live on one's own terms, being less dependent on God, could not wholly smother the spirit in him, and a new form of humanism emerged out of the two warring forces of Christianity. This process of the evolution of new humanism is a part of historical process governed by Hegelian dialectics, 'thesis-anti-thesis-synthesis'; every thesis has seeds of antithesis in it which, while destroying it, sprouts in the form of synthesis, leading to a new thesis and so on. Anthropocentrism was eventually overcome by synthesis of faith and unfaith which is 'the middle state'. Man was fully aware of the hazards of extremity and made reintegration the ultimate strategy of survival to live by.

In the Renaissance, the words 'humanist' and 'humanism' were used in a distinct technical sense: a student of the humanistic discipline was called a 'humanist' and his study was designated as 'humanism'. The moderns today seem to concentrate more on its literal meaning as the Dictionary defines "a person having a strong interest or concerned for human welfare, values and dignity", rather than on what it was used in the beginning in the 13th century or the Renaissance humanists used in the 15th century in England. And the manner in which they view humanism appears near to the philosophy of humanitarianism which is defined as "a doctrine that mankind may become perfect without divine aid" or "that man's obligation are concerned wholly with the welfare of the human race". This is seen in the four features that the contemporary humanists emphasize in their understanding of humanism which Paul Kurtz has enlisted as under.

> First, Humanists have some confidence in man and they believe that the only bases for morality are human experience and human needs. Second, many or most Humanists are opposed to all forms of supernaturalistic and authoritarian religion. Third, many Humanists believe that scientific intelligence and critical reason can assist in reconstructing our moral values. And fourth, Humanism is humanitarian in that it is concerned with the good life and social justice as moral ideals.[48]

But the problem in the acceptance of such a view is that it takes the discussion out of the range and scope of the project in the sense that humanism, as the moderns have understood, includes a wide diversity of the humanist viewpoint and the classical notion of humanism which is marked by its range of 'scholarship' and 'learning' ceases to be a distinctive term. The various schools of humanism may differ in their approach to and study of man in relation to God and universe, nevertheless what saves their view from being a tower of Babel are the concerns for human dignity and commitment to moral sense which is summed up in the slogan "Everything is for Man" and thus there is no wonder if they find church rituals wanting for their failure to promote good life, and need reorientation to make them relevant to human needs. However, the humanitarians' less emphasis on divine intervention is perhaps to confute the 'littleness of man' as espoused by the nihilistic theoreticians and not to deny God. The belief that moral values be divorced from the framework of theology and "that our moral ideals must be constantly re-examined and revised in the light of present needs and demands" is less an espousal of the anthropocentric view of the universe and more an admission of the truth that the ideals of good life, social justice and morality can be equally realised by continuing to living with God.

Paul Kurtz identifies humanism with 'moral revolution' for its showing concern with the ideals of ethics and morality which connects him with the attitude of the Renaissance humanists towards Christianity and paganism, the aim being to reconcile the ancient and the Christian ideas "in the manner of Erasmus". The humanists were not dogmatic on moral, religious and theological problems, they made use of the hidden meaning in the pagan stories to fit it into Christian thought the impact of which is seen on the moral thought of the Renaissance. All this shows that "Renaissance humanism as a whole cannot be identified with a particular set of opinion or convictions but is rather characterized by a cultural ideal and range of scholarly, literary, and intellectual interests that the individual humanist was able to combine with a variety of professional, philosophical and theological convictions".[49]

The two most common assumptions in the contemporary notion of humanism are: first, the value of human potential and second, the rejection of any system of thought, like nihilism which denies any meaning to life and generates feelings of pessimism and meaninglessness and which treats man as depraved only to be saved by divine grace. The humanists of today have also shown that humanism has its affinity with the philosophy of existentialism: as humanism renders man truly human so does the doctrine of existentialism "renders human life possible". What is central in the two philosophies is the creation of consciousness in man that he has human dignity and power which he has to respect and cultivate in his ownself and promote the same in others as well. This aspect of value finds expression in Sartrean concept of human subjectivity and the ontology of the Being which makes man a 'project'.

> Man first of all exists encounters himself, surges up in the world and defines himself afterwards... man is not definable, it is because he is nothing. He will not be anything until latter and then he will be what he makes of himself. Man is not what he conceives to be, but is what he wills and makes of himself.[50]

There is a stress on the fusion of the value of the self and responsibility and commitment. The humanists look upon man as a "goal-seeking organism", and discourages individualism in the pursuit of seeking fulfillment: his values cannot be arbitrary, rather they are to be grounded in the realities of human situation, its need and history. "The ethical Humanist finds his 'golden mean' in an earth-born, life-centred and realistic ethic-open, emphatic, pragmatic and non-exclusive enabling us to avoid the extremes of absolutism and nihilism which are alike corrosive of meaningful freedom and responsibility".[51]

Horace L. Friess's definition of humanism stresses the value of human dignity, power and a sense of responsibility which are essential "for achieving an integrity and wholeness of human life". John Herman Randall Jr.'s comment[52] on Friess's definition further brings under focus the humanist's programme which includes "(i) an emphasis on power and dignity of man, on the worth of human personality, (ii) on the obligation to respect and cultivate that dignity and worth in oneself and in others, (iii) on responsibility, on self control, on self-direction towards integrity and wholeness as the foundation on which the others rest". Agreed that responsibility is central and man in certain human sense is free. But does freedom deny God? They protest against man's subservience to any external authority, religious or mechanical, imposed upon man from without. But the use of the word 'obligation' suggests that man is not wholly free, rather "obligation is a curtailment of the freedom to do wrong".[53]

The humanist insistence on "the autonomy of the moral life" is in accord with the rise of moral consciousness that enables man to transcend his finite ends and inadequacies to assure the intactness of his humanity.

The humanist's view that man cannot live without hope and faith implies the idea of creation of value which no one can lose sight of but the question is what form of humanism, theistic or atheistic is the source of value and whether the values will ensure victory. And second if human mind has its own limitations to make sense of the world around him beyond a point, does the situation as such not generate feelings of meaninglessness or despair? Humanism thus, if seen in its modernistic framework does not destroy realism, nor does it profess to claim that man is perfect or perfectable. But in the existing situation it certainly holds man "responsible for his uses of the knowledge and the power he has won through thousand of years of intelligent study of his environment". Thus, the philosophy of humanism, as interpreted today, is the philosophy of theocentric humanism the basis of which is hope and faith and man should proceed with an open mind on the problem of ontology. It makes no false promises either. Therefore, it is unwise to be sceptical about man's essential nobility. At heart, man is passionately a moral being and feels happy to see evil overthrown. But it is true that the value to be human lies in what direction our striving is stretched to. If what we dream of self and society is not realized, it is the result of false humanism and therefore in the existing situation the despair or nihilism would also not carry us too far. This is how we begin to understand the complexities of life and learn to live by following a philosophy of reintegration between knowledge and faith.

The faith which Camus declares in *The Myth of Sisyphus* that "even within the limits of nihilism it is possible to find the means to proceed beyond nihilism" is not anchored in man's anthropocentric view of the universe. Camus is the singer of the positivistic aspect of absurdity. If the universe is absurd even then it is a universe man has to live *in* it, not *over* it which implies the acquiescense of the divine plan and live in according with its dictates as Thoreau philosophises in the *Walden.* It is this that frees man from illusions to be his own God. Some modern thinkers are of the view that there is nothing for man to look beyond human intellect and power of reason to fall back upon in moments of crisis. "Man stands on his own feet without fear of punishment or promise of reward. Man makes his own Hell and his own Heaven and he makes it here and now."[54] In other words, their view of reality is bound by 'this worldliness'. There is no world, they think, beyond it and if there is any future it lies within, not outside. But to deny the medieval notion of 'other worldliness' and say that man can create heaven and hell 'here and now' is a serious flaw which by no means will make man to fully realize himself. In the words of H.J. Blackham, humanism is a human programme based on certain intrinsic values of life for ameliorating human lot.

> Acceptance of interdependence and the solidarity of interests as the basis of human relations means acceptance of a share in joint responsibility for creating for all the conditions of a life worthy to be called human, a human providence in which each may be his own and without mockery.[55]

Thus, keeping in view man's encounter with the self and his response to the complex of choices of 'free and unfree acts' which defines his humanity, the moderns lay emphasis on humanism's existential value. That is it "attempts to provide a coherent answer to the questions of human existence and assumes that existence can be made worthwhile by the realization of everyone's possibilities in devotion to a common humanity".[56] Contrary to it, Marlovian heroes are highly individualistic, committed to the cult of self and ignore the interest of common humanity. The humanist concept of morality and its emphasis on the "autonomy of the moral life" is alien to their nature for the fact that their moral vision is destroyed by false humanism and thus evolves no philosophy of survival, nor has it any direction outside the romantic liberation of self. This is one reason that their morality clashes with the modern notion of humanist morality which is "based on the acknowledgement of the mutual solidarity of men and their equivalence in the consideration of their interest and aspirations, it is directed towards the maturity of all men".[57] The truth is that they seem to share the humanist's belief, as Marlowe does, that "man is his own end" but they are unaware of its ironic implications that if the ends are open, it does not mean that everything is permissible. The grand project they undertake ironically robs them of their humanness and the comicality of the whole thing is that they are hardly aware of it.

M.M. Mahood has convincingly shown the fall of the humanist ideal as projected in Marlowe's plays in four successive stages, which are: (i) assertion of self-sufficiency verging on utopia (*Tamburlaine*), (ii) seeking wilful separation from the divine source to be godhead and thus meeting, in state of spiritual rootlessness, eternal damnation (*Faustus*), (iii) man's conversion into a dragon as a result of his worship of sham gods of mercantilism and ending in the cauldron of his own passion of lust and crime (*The Jew of Malta*) and (iv) the denial of life, a craving of death, contrary to the humanist emphasis on the value of living (*Edward II*). Tamburlaine, the protagonist of Marlowe's first play, is the creation of the dramatist's this Elizabethan experience of the tragic urge of the time. Being drugged by the dreamy vision of self-sufficiency, Tamburlaine oversteps limitations to the extent of allowing God no part to play in human existence and be the 'Scourge of God'. But could he become so? His last words

'Tamburlaine, the scourge of God, must die'

are a travesty of the grand project he undertakes to measure his strength against nature and be law unto himself. Faustus is a powerful illustration and exemplification of the 'misdirected desire', he is left lonely in his last minute strife to escape a fate he is destined to meet. Barabas is another creation of the abuse of human intellect and spiritual potentialities. He falls a prey to an all-pervading mercantile instinct of the time and wields the power of fabulous wealth as Tamburlaine does sword power to control a Christian state he is planted in. The God he invokes is the money-God who, he believes, will set everything in motion by its force of mercantilism which fails him in crucial moments when he most needs its help. The boiling cauldron becomes symbolically the sea that drowned the Phonecian sailor, Phalebas. The final stage of the self-destructive tendency in humanism is projected in *Edward II* which is "the denial, not only of human spirituality and greatness but of life itself." Edward's craving for death in prison is not a move to deherocize the hero but it is a step toward complete nihiliation of what man is endowed with and what is stressed in humanism. As a king, he should have risen to the Renaissance ideal of sovereignty to serve as a moral touchstone for others to envy but the point, he debases himself to, shows that evil lies in man, not in system, rank or social position.

But Marlowe is well aware of the question which the humanists encounter regarding the morality of value and choice—whether the choices man makes are within human control? He does not impose any value pattern upon them from his own, nor does he support their philosophy of action limited to self-aggrandizement, machiavellian opportunism overambitiousness and craziness for power, rather he wholly leaves them free in the pursuit of their wish for goal for us to see whether we accept or reject it.

Marlowe is thus the first analyst of the moral decay set in the Renaissance. His plays, by implication, are a paradigm of a counter value structure which discourages the extreme anti-humanist view of things in theological concerns, so that man may stay human. His diagnosis of this moral malaise and the anatomy of nature in its inevitability of striving after power and pleasure is prophetic in the sense that, if the striving tends to be erring and individualistic, it leads to nihilating the very notion of humanism. Marlowe's departure from the Athenian tragedy in certain matters further underlines his philosophy of art and life. The point is not, as to how much he owes to classical tragedy in regard to projecting the tragic dilemma of his age on the stage, but how he looks upon the contemporary scene in the 16th century England from the viewpoint of a tragic artist and how it finds reflection in his plays. He is a realist but he "does not invent his characters to fit into his moral judgements" he shows in his plays on a broader canvas what man is and how he acts and reacts in a given situation to find himself. A situation is created which by nature is what human heart longs for but which is also a test of his humanity, hard for one to resist. That is why he wrote tragedies, not comedies to project his view of man and by dramatizing the interplay of human passions at various levels such as greed, lust for power and gold, sensuality, revenge, rivalry and senseless violence which led to the disintegration of humanism, he has shown how during the process man is divested of self-esteem and is driven to hell or to a boiling cauldron for his failure to seek integration between the benefits of 'new learning' and medieval fatalism.

NOTES

1. Harry Levin, *Christopher Marlowe: The Overreacher*, London: Faber and Faber Ltd., 1952, p. 18.
2. Fredrick S. Boas, *Christopher Marlowe: A Biographical and Critical Study*, Oxford: The Clarenden Press, 1940, p. 109.
3. *Idem.*
4. *Ibid.*, p. 100.
5. The term 'Atheist' for the first time is known in connection with Marlowe in Robert Greene's Preface to *Perimedes the Blacksmith* (1588).

   > ...daring God out of heaven with that Atheist Tamburlaine, followed by the sneer at 'mad and scoffing poets, that have prophetical spirits as bred of Merlins race'.

   Greene was Marlowe's senior at Cambridge by two years. He was envious of the younger man's triumph in the theatre while his own only venture as yet was "to palter up something in Prose". Marlowe was often known by the name of the wizard Marlin. Greene's insinuation is apparent to attack Marlowe as the writer of *Tamburlaine.*

   (Quoted in Frederick S. Boas, p. 111)
6. *Ibid.*, p. 109.
7. *Ibid.*, p. 260.

8. *Ibid.*, p. 262. Boas quotes one passage wherein Mephostophilis tells Faustus that the banishment from God's presence is in itself damnation.

   Why, this is hell, nor am I out of it.
   Think'st thou that I that saw the face of God
   And tasted the eternal joys of heaven,
   Am not tormented with ten thousand hells
   In being deprived of everlasting bliss?
   (*Doctor Faustus*, Act I, Sc. iii)

9. *Idem.*

10. *Idem.*

11. *Idem.*

12. Harry Levin, *Christopher Marlowe: The Overreacher*, *op.* cit., p. 19.

13. Frederick S. Boas, *Christopher Marlowe: A Biographical and Critical Study*, *op. cit.*, p. 250.

14. Greene's exhortation is to those wits making plays. Of the five gentlemen, he first singles out Marlowe, the expression is more of sorrow, instead of anger.

    Wonder not (for with thee will I first begin) thou famous gracer of Tragedians, that Greene who hath said with thee like the foole in his heart, there is no God, should now giue glorie into this greatness: for penetrating in his power, his hand lies heauie upon me, he hath spoken into me with a voice of thunder, and I have felt he is a God that can punish enemies. Why should thy excellent wit, his gift, be so blinded, that thou should giue no glory to the giuer?
    (Frederick S. Boas, p. 238)

15. Marlin (i.e. Marlowe), by profession a scholar, brought up from his youth in the University of Cambridge but by practice a playmaker and a poet of scurrility who, by giving too large a swinge to his own wit and suffering his lust to have the full reins, fell not without just desert, to that outrage and extremity that he denied God and his son Christ, and not only in word blasphemed the Trinity but also (as it is credibly reported) wrote books against it, affirming our Saviour to be but a deceiver, and Moses to be but a conjurer and seducer of the people, and the Holy Bible to be but vain and idle stories, and all religion but a device of policy (pp. 147-48).

(From Thomas Beard's *Theatre of God's Judgements* (1597) Quoted in the Introduction to *Christopher Marlowe* ed. by David Bevington and Eric Rasmussen, p. viii).

16. *Ibid.*, p. ix.
17. Frederick S. Boas, *Christopher Marlowe: A Biographical and Critical Study*, *op. cit.*, p. 259.
18. Epicureanism is a philosophical system of the Greek philosopher, Epicurus (342?-270 BC). The philosophy of Epicureanism was a threat to the church for its interference in the concept of an 'after life', second its emphasis on intellectual pleasure being the summum bonum of human life, opposed to the medieval notion of extreme asceticism and self denial was accepted less a condemnatory verdict in the Renaissance.
19. Machiavelli was an ardent republican and anti-clerical. Why did he write a kind of book as *The Prince* which was banned but its circulation continued so clandestinely? Garrat Mattingly in a brilliant article on Machiavelli in J.H. Plumb's *The Penguin Book of the Renaissance* gives two reasons: (i) to damn the soul and ruin the fortunes of the princes who followed it, (ii) to warn all free men of the dangers of tyranny. In the 18th century, it was read as a satire on absolute monarchy for its anti-authoritarian overtones.
20. Paul Oskar Kristeller, *Renaissance Thought II: Papers on Humanism and the Arts*, New York: Harper and Row Publishers, 1965, p. 2.
21. *Ibid.*, p. 20.
22. Naresh Chandra, *The Literature of the English Renaissance*, Delhi: Doaba Publishing House, 1985, p. 16.
23. J.H. Plumb, *The Penguin Book of the Renaissance*, Penguin Books Ltd., 1964, pp. 21-22.
24. Quoted in *The Literature of the English Renaissance*, *op. cit.*, p. 14.
25. H.B. Parkes, "Nature's Diverse Laws: The Double Vision of the Elizabethans", *Sewanee Review*, LVIII, 1950, pp. 403-04. Quoted in *Landmarks in Modern English Literature*.
26. *The Penguin Book of the Renaissance*, *op. cit.*, p. 22.
27. Gordon Campbell (ed.) *Macmillan Anthologies of English Literature: The Renaissance (1550-1660)*, Vol. II, London: Macmillan Education Ltd., 1989, p. XIX.

28. Quoted by Rev. J. Wylie in *History of Protestantism*, Vol. I, p. 53 from M. Crie's *Progress and Supression in Italy*, 1833, p. 41 in *The Literature of the English Renaissance*, p. 8.

29. Jack F. Bernard, *Italy: An Historical Survey*, p. 243. Quoted in *The Literature of the English Renaissance*, p. 14.

30. Paul Oskar Kristeller, *Renaissance Thought: The Classic, Scholastic and Humanist Strains*, New York: Harper Torchbooks, 1961, pp. 120-21.

31. Paul Oskar Kristeller, *Renaissance Thought: Papers on Humanism and the Arts*, *op. cit.*, p. 2.

32. *Ibid.*, p. 23.

33. *Ibid.*, p. 24.

34. A professional teacher or a student of these subjects was called 'humanista', the term 'humanist' came to be used in documents in the late 15th century and became common during the 16th century.

35. E. Garin, *Per Italienische Humanismus*, Berlin, 1947. Quoted in Paul Oskar Kristeller, *Renaissance Thought: The Classic, Scholastic and Humanist Strains*, *op. cit.*, p. 9.

36. Many Italian scholars entered the service of foreign princes or dignitaries, as tutors or secretaries, as librarians, as court poets or court historians. The list is long and distinguished, and it includes Aeneas Sylvius in Germany, Antonius Bonfinius in Hungary, Philippus Callimachus in Poland, Poggio, Titus Livius Frulovisius and Polydore Vergil in England, Paulus Aemilius in France, Lucius Marineus Siculus and Petrus Martyr Anglariensis in Spain.

    (Paul Oskar Kristeller, p. 74)

37. *Ibid.*, pp. 75-76.

    A famous early example is Cola di Rienzo whose short stay in Bohemia left some significant traces. In the late 15th century, Philippus Callimachus came to Poland as a political exile, and gradually attained a position of great cultural and political importance at the court of Cracow. In the 16th century, the Protestant exiles from Italy who went especially to Switzerland, England and Poland included many highly educated scholars. Pellegrino Morato and his daughter Olimpia went from Ferrara to Germany. In Basel, Italian Protestant scholars worked as authors and editors in close connection with the flourishing book trade. The most famous of the group was Celio Secundo Curione from Venice.

38. Quoted in M.M. Mahood, *Poetry and Humanism*, London: The Camelot Press Ltd., 1958, p. 12.
39. *Ibid.*, p. 19.
40. *Ibid.*, p. 13.
41. Miriam Allen de Ford, "Heretical Humanism" in *The Humanist Alternative: Some Definitions of Humanism*, p. 81.
42. *Poetry and Humanism*, p. 14.
43. "Thus is Man that great and true Amphibium whose nature is disposed to live, nor only like other creatures in divers elements but in divided and distinguished worlds." Quoted in *Poetry and Humanism*.
44. Crane Brinton, *The Shaping of Modern Mind*, New York: A Mentor Book, 1983, p. 43.
45. Jacob Burckhardt, *The Civilisation of the Renaissance Italy*, Oxford: Phaeton Press, 1945, p. 162.
46. *Poetry and Humanism*, *op. cit.*, p. 14.
47. Emile Brehiere, *The Middle Ages and the Renaissance*, London, Chicago: The University of Chicago Press, 1967, pp. 217-18. Quoted in V.K. Roy, *Landmarks in Modern English Literature*, New Delhi: Kanishka Publications, 1999, p. 13.
48. Paul Kurtz, "Humanism and the Moral Revolution", *The Humanist Alternative: Some Definitions of Humanism*, *op. cit.*, p. 49.
49. *Renaissance Thought II: Papers on Humanism and the Arts*, *op. cit.*, p. 40.
50. J.P. Sarte, *Existentialism and Humanism*, trans. by Philip Mairet, Methuen and Co., 1970, p. 28.
51. Edward L. Ericson, "Ethical Humanism" in *The Humanist Alternative: Some Definitions of Humanism*, *op. cit.*, p. 56.
52. John Herman Randall Jr., "What is the Temper of Humanism?" in *The Humanist Alternative: Some Definitions of Humanism*, *op. cit.*, p. 58.
53. *Ibid.*, p. 59.

54. Algernon D. Black, "Our Quest for Faith: Is Humanism Enough" in *The Humanist Alternative: Some Definitions of Humanism*, *op. cit.*, p. 77.
55. H.J. Blackham, "A Definition of Humanism", in *The Humanist Alternative: Some Definitions of Humanism*, *op. cit.*, p. 36.
56. J.P. Van Praag, "What is Humanism" in *The Humanist Alternative: Some Definitions of Humanism*, *op. cit.*, p. 45.
57. *Idem.*

2

Tamburlaine Part First

The Renaissance is stated to be the "Middle Ages minus God", Paul Oskar Kristeller denies the charge saying that he finds no Renaissance thinker turning indifferent to God. They did believe in a God but what God they believed in is a different story. If Marlowe's heroes dare to usurp the divine authority, it is their subjective imprisonment, not of Marlowe's and the phase is otherwise ephemeral because what at the end becomes triumphant is the spirit of theocentric humanism. The fact is illustrated by what happens to Tamburlaine in two parts.

One positive gain of the Renaissance is the growth of self consciousness as revealed by the discoveries and explorations which, when perverted to the point even of allowing God no part to play in human existence, including life and death, ends in life's negation which is a sure symptom of the disintegration of the humanist ideal. How comical that the man who once proclaimed holding "the Fates bound fast in iron chains" and "turn Fortune's wheel about" meets his failure, first in Zenocrate's death and then finally in his own with the words "For Tamburlaine, the Scourage of God must die!" The fatal contradiction is apparent. Humanism, as Maritain maintains, "tends to render man truly human" and brings out the original greatness by making him participate in all "that can enrich him in nature and history". One wonders what mark of greatness, the Scythian warrior intends to attain the hollowness of which becomes manifest during his ride in the two parts of the play.

Marlowe's choice of 'Tamburlaine subject', so different from the themes of classical, Italian or British origin which were the source material for comedy or tragic-comedy in England, owes to his Cambridge studies and translations of Latin poetry.[1] With his entry into the pre-Shakespearean drama, there was a radical change in the presentation of the tragic spectacle of life on the stage. The medieval concept of tragedy was looked upon as a loose concept of tragedy for its weakness to bring out the heroic in man that makes the tragic action in Aristotelian sense, illuminating, not depressing.

History shows Tamburlaine as a bandit-chief, a common Scythian shepherd by origin and the problem was how to carve out of the source material a character of heroic stature but it was overcome by placing the study of man in the context of the Renaissance ethos of inordinate lust for power. What interested Marlowe was a spirit struggling to rise above the average level of humanity and measure out its powers against limitations to the utmost degree but not at the cost of the divorce between the natural and the spiritual man. Marlowe had a great faith in man's potentialities but he was also conscious of the moral hazards if they are put to disuse. Tamburlaine is a case of deluded self, he scoffs at the idea of the celestial powers crushing man at will and proclaims himself as a lord who holds "the Fates fast bound in iron chains".[2]

The Prologue announces the entry of Tamburlaine with carefully chosen words which, when the play was published anonymous, were written on the title page by the publishers. It tells the audience in high sounding terms about his race and wonderful conquests by which he became "a mighty monarch and for his tyranny and terror in war was termed the Scourage of God". The two words 'terror' and 'tyranny' in the Prologue evoke images of power-game of which man became conscious in Renaissance England which was suppressed in the Middle Ages.

Humanism does not deny the value of man but lest the expression that man is the measure of all things be not an exercise in self-defeating subjectivity, it emphasizes the 'automomy of the moral life' and holds man fully responsible for what he does or what he makes of himself. Frederick S. Boas observes that the Renaissance, age was intoxicated by the magnificent possibilities, opened to it on every side and thus the distinguishing note was "an uncontrollable aspiration after the ideal, a scorn of earthly conditions, a soaring passion that sought to scale the infinitudes of power, beauty, thought and love".[3] It finds nowhere more a characteristic vent, the critic contends, than in Marlowe's Tamburlaine—the thirst for limitless power.

The Prologue's assurance to the audience that they—

> shall hear the Scythian Tamburlaine
> Threatening the world with high astounding terms
> And scourging kingdoms with his conquering sword.[4]

—at once connects the young dramatist's soaring imagination with an aspiring warrior's aim of realization of the ideal in the sphere of creative will. One wonders whether the dramatization of overreaching ideas, which were never presented on the stage before, are of Marlowe or of Tamburlaine whose conquest he has chosen to dramatize? The very first words, Tamburlaine speaks, tell about his humble origin, "a shepherd by my parentage" and reflect the height his mind is set to scale. Tamburlaine's world under threat is historical, having a concrete stretch of geographical territories and its expansion and shrinkage is rather a terror of history but Marlower's world is certainly a world of Christian orthodoxy and a slight upheaval or departure from the norms of conventional morality makes his position dubious.

Thus, the stage is set for some upheaval to take place. We wait for the mighty monarch to appear in "complete armour and this curtle-axe" which are, he feels, "adjuncts more beseeming Tamburlaine".[5] But what instead we see is that the stage is occupied by a different person, the Persian King, Mycetes who happens to be an inefficient and nerveless ruler, the very anti-thesis of the Scythian Tamburlaine. A contrary set of value is brought into the play with Mycetes's anti-war strain: "Accurs'd be he that first invented war". He is a forerunner of Edward-II who happens to be the king but has little kingliness about him. Marlowe exploits this weakness, partly to project Tamburlaine's chivalry and partly to show that it is not the rank or the position that makes one a hero but the heroic veins and passion to challenge nature one is endowed with. It is not that the image of Mycetes as a king is deherocised as a device of episodic intensification to make Tamburlaine's rise possible on his inefficiency but it is partly an expression of Marlowe's scorn for the weakness in the person of the king who himself makes confession of his being a lesser wit to his brother, "Cosroe: I know you have a better wit than I".[6]

Mycetes' weakness is made more glaring by Cosroe, who calls Persia 'unhappy' for being ruled and governed by a man

> At whose birthday Cynthia with Saturn join'd,
> And Jove, the Sun, and Mercury denied
> To shed their influence in his fickle brain.
> Now Turks and Tartars shake their swords at thee,
> Meaning to mangle all thy provinces.[7]

Mycetes feels offended to hear the truth about him, being told in such a free and frank manner. But his own part in the creation of such an unheroic image of a king cannot be overlooked. His own confession, "I am not wise enough to be a king", is much amusing verging on the technique of self-mockery but despite this ironic awareness he happens to be the king. The cause of his grief is Tamburlaine's entry into Persia which, he feels, is a threat to his very existence. The instinct of living is alive in him but the commensurate courage and efforts to sustain it are lacking which makes the whole claim ridiculous: "but yet I know I might/ yet live, yea, live; Mycetes wills it so". Perhaps Mycetes is not conscious of the implication of the words he uses to condemn Tamburlaine's 'fox-like' conduct which is a sort of glorification of his valour vis-à-vis his Persian soldiers whom he equates with a herd of innocent animals.

> Like a fox in midst of harvest-time,
> Doth prey upon my flocks of passengers;
> And, as I hear, doth mean to pull my plumes.[8]

Critics hear a prophetic alarm in the words "harvest time", suggesting a ripe time for Mycetes' destruction. Tamburlaine is introduced by Meander as the 'sturdy Scythian thief who robs merchants and daily commits 'in civil outrages' hoping

> To reign in Asia, and with barbarous arms
> To make himself the monarch of the East:[9]

Meander's advice to entrust charge of Tamburlaine's arrest to Theridamas which is in a way a proxy-war is hardly a kingly resolution, rather it shows him less a man of action and depending more on the illusion created by the magic of the words. Theridamas's heroic proclamation is a display of the extravagance of diction which was a common sin of the time but misplaced in the existing situation.

> Before the moon renew her borrow'd light,
> Doubt not, my lord and gracious sovereign,
> But Tamburlaine and that Tartarian rout
> Shall either perish by our warlike hands,
> Or plead for mercy at your highness' feet.[10]

The words have the sharpness of the edge of the sword, "thy words are swords", says Mycetes and in the dispatch of Theridamas to the field, he harbours the fond hopes of victory over the enemy which is a high piece of comedy. In imagination, he sees the white horses, besmeared with blood and laden with human heads, symbolic of triumph, he calls it a dainty show but we know that the reality is otherwise. For a coward, like Mycetes the sight of horses carrying human heads cannot be a feast to the eye. The truth is that it is sufficient to evoke shudder, rather than creating a stir in his stagnant pools.

> I long to see thee back return from thence,
> That I may view these milk-white steeds of mine
> All loaden with the heads of killed men,
> And from their knees even to their hoofs below
> Besmear'd with blood that makes a dainty show.[11]

Tamburlaine appears accompanied by lords and Zenocrate,[12] the daughter of the king of Egypt, who once was betrothed to the king of Arabia and to whom Tamburlaine has made captive. The procession is characteristic of the

Renaissance fondness for pomp and glory. As the action advances we learn that Tamburlaine has the full support of his followers who vie with each other to shower the extravagant praise on him. The praise, so lavishly showered on Tamburlaine, is the triumph of Marlowe's artistry but it has its socio-historical context: in the Elizabethan and the Jacobean age there was a rat-race among the courtiers to win the favour of the crown. The dimensions of terror associated with Tamburlaine are further painted by his follower, Techelles in a dreamy vision, the imagery is fully functional.

> As princely lions, when they rouse themselves,
> Stretching their paws, and threatening herds of beasts
> So in his armour looketh Tamburlaine.
> Methinks I see kings kneeling at his feet,
> And he with frowning brows and fiery looks
> Spurning their crowns from off their captive heads.[13]

Tamburlaine's humble birth is no obstacle to rise high because his philosophy, as it was of Marlowe's as well, is the philosophy of action: it is not the birth but deeds performed which create in the existential sense, the authenticity and the concreteness of the Being. That is why he does not feel ashamed of his parentage and proclaims himself as 'a lord', despite being a shepherd by birth.

> I am a lord, for so my deeds shall prove,
> And yet a shepherd by my parentage.[14]

Humanism does not see any wrong if self-discovery impels man to be a lord on earth but it condemns his defiance and usurption of the divine authority which is a violation of the division of power between man and gods. Tamburlaine uses a highly suggestive spatial imagery to impress upon Zenocrate's mind his 'empery' which is a triumph of the alchemy of eloquence outside his physical powers. Finding no apt object to compare within the world of men, he turns to the world of nature, he likens the limitlessness of his exploits with the course of the sun that it measures east and west across the vast stretch of the blueness of the sky.

And means to be terror to the world,
Measuring the limits of his empery
By east and west, as Phoebus doth his course.[15]

The urge of being a superman in Tamburlaine by virtue of deeds, in Nietzschean sense, has nothing immoral about it. Morality for him is power-morality. There is an upward thrust in man as in nature, an evolutionary urge to be what one is not. But the wrong lies wherein the urge loses moral sense and is rendered purposeless. The tragic flaw Tamburlaine suffers from is the imperfect knowing of self that generates in him a desire for limitless power but what the dramatist seems to suggest is that even in limitlessness there are limitations which man should know and accept to stay human. He never talks of doing something worthwhile for the benefit of mankind in general even when after the conquests he happens to be the monarch of the Eastern world which shows that his desire constitutes for the sake of desire.

It is the unresistable spell of Marlowe's poetic powers which find expression in Tamburlaine's personality. He makes a 45 line speech having Milotonic majesty to impress on the enemy's mind his individuality the Renaissance man became aware of. The medieval notion 'destiny is character' is replaced by the new dictum which is 'character is destiny' when man refused to be overawed by the celestial powers and occupied the central stage in the scheme of things. Tamburlaine refuses to admit any limitations on freedom and the obstacles to the realization of the ideal he sets out to attain.

It so happens that Theridamas, the Persian Commander, is sent with a 'thousand horse men' to fight 'five hundred foot' Scythian soldiers. The colonialist construct of Tamburlaine seems to have a good understanding of human psychology and knows how to win secretly loyalties even of the enemy. Tamburlaine, as a matter of truth, is a personification of the forces of divisiveness and disunity, contrary to the humanistic value of "the mutual solidarity of all men".[16] He calls Theridamas 'mighty man-at-arms' and tells him how in case of assault on him, Jove himself will "stretch his hand from heaven/ To ward the blow, and shield me safe from harm".[17]

Tamburlaine persuades the Persian to join hands so that the two could attain godhood. The description of Jove in pastoral imagery has psychological implications. When Jove in 'shepherd's weed' can scale the heavens, why not they?

Jove sometimes masked in a shepherd's weed
And by those steps that he hath scal'd the heavens
May we become immortal like the gods.[18]

Tamburlaine's strategy works and Theridamas stands charmed like a child in a fairy land. No arms are drawn, no battle is fought, even then Theridamas accepts defeat, surprisingly enough, not by the power of weaponary but of words. He yields to Tamburlaine with his men and horses to share his fortune—good or bad.

And Tamburlaine like a shrewd calculating victor traps the emissary into a highly improbable illusion which extends beyond the earthly limits "And both our souls aspire celestial thrones" when their bodies turn to elements. This is his false humanism. M.M. Mahood says that the musician Orpheus overcame death through the enchantment of his symphony: "the Tamburlaine of these opening scenes is essentially Orphic". However, it is not only Theridamas alone who is won over by the power of his eloquence but Cosroe who later betrays Myectes is another to fall in the line, though one can see in it the Machiavellian opportunism and the Renaissance lust for power to be himself the king of Persia under the regency of Tamburlaine.

In fair Persia noble Tamburlaine
Shall be my regent and remain as king.[19]

As a matter of truth, the world of Tamburlaine is a Renaissance world wherein all are engaged in the pursuit of power game. Cosroe relishes wearing crown, the Turkish emperor, Bajazeth, is engaged in war in Europe. Tamburlaine being a Renaissance man, enters this world and dictates his own terms by translating ambition into action and if others fail to do so, it is for the lack of their will power. Cosroe's march against Mycetes, the rightful king of Persia and calling the Persian army the 'fainting army of that foolish king' is a case of deluded self caught in the vortex of lust for power. The Persian army is defeated and Cosroe is crowned as the new king of Persia by Ortygius, Menaphon and others who earlier were loyal to Mycetes. It is not that Tamburlaine alone is swept away by the taste of power, but it percolates into the lower ranks which the dramatist so artistically captures in the shifting scale of loyalty of those who crown Cosroe as a king. But later Tamburlaine turns against him and the new dignity conferred on him is snatched away. Cosroe feels his sense of nobility and pride injured and thus accuses Tamburlaine of betrayal and mistrust. His reproaches are weak to move the "Bloody and insatiate Tamburlaine". What moved Tamburlaine to take arms against Persia is "the thirst of reign and the sweetness of a crown". He justifies his action by referring to the treatment meted out to Saturn by Jove which is an expression of a wishful thought that he is Jove among the men, risen above the average level of humanity by sheer force of character and victory and has the right to treat men as he will. He claims to have that mysterious urge and passion for sovereignty that, no doubt, moves all men to aspiring ideals but all are not endowed with that extraordinary nature which, he feels, he is born with. Thus, he acts as Marlowe's mouthpiece while measuring his strength against commonality.

> What better precedent that might Jove?
> Nature, that fram'd us of four elements
> Warring within our breasts for regiment,
> Doth teach us all to have aspiring minds.
> Our souls, whose faculties can comprehend
> The wondrous architecture of the world,
> And measure every wandering planet's course,
> Still climbing after knowledge infinite,
> And always moving as the restless spheres,
> Wills us to wear ourselves and never rest,
> Until we reach the ripest fruit of all,
> That perfect bliss and sole felicity,
> The sweet fruition of an earthy crown.[20]

With Cosroe's defeat and death, Tamburlaine is crowned as the king of Persia with the approval of all. "Long live Tamburlaine, and reign in Asia". He sees in it a sort of divine glorification and greets this popular acclamation and assent of all the warring lords with a sense of satisfaction.

> So; now it is more surer on my head
> Than if the gods had held a parliament,
> And all pronunc'd me king of Persia.[21]

After the fall of the state of Persia being a 'decadent royal house', Tamburlaine is drugged with a surfeit of power which comes on the fore in the fight with the Turkish emperor, Bajazeth. Bajazeth is not Mycetes. Marlowe highlights his might, putting it against Tamburlaine's. Bajazeth is painted as

> Dread lord of Afric, Europe and Asia,
> Great king and conqueror of Graecia,
> The ocean, Terrene, and the Coal-blacksea,
> The high and highest monarch of the world.[22]

which is no doubt a might that cannot be undermined but it is weak and ineffectual to outmatch Tamburlaine's glory who is "term'd the Scourage and Wrath of God and terror of the world".[23]

Passages as such bear testimony to the fact that Tamburlaine is Marlowe's first hero, cast into the mould of the values which the false humanism that ran parallel to the true humanism in the Renaissance prized most. The captive kings in Part Second do not get a human treatment. They are forcibly yoked to drag the chariot to the next battlefield. What does it suggest? Or in what way does it add to his glory? As a matter of fact, it is the overdose of hysteria, as generated by power and gold, the evil impact of which has corroded the finer values of life in Tamburlaine. The show of ride over human steeds is less a demonstration of power to create scare in the mind of the enemy and more a reflection of man's inhumanity to man and sadism. Such scenes of savagery diminish what the Part One shows ending in triumph and glory and what the epigraph spoken by Amyras at the end of Part Two tells about his surpassing the glory of earth and heaven.

> Let earth and heaven his timeless death deplore,
> For both their worths will equal him no more![24]

What happens after Bajazeth's defeat and capture is less an attestation of the power play of Tamburlaine and more a show of primitive savagery and utter disregard to human values. Theridamas plucks away the crown from Zabina's head and gives it to Zenocrate saying "Here, Madam, you are empress, she is none" which is a vulgar display of the lust for gold but an accepted value in the world of the play. At his command, they are bound in chains like animals in herd. The royal couple is helpless and, being God-fearing, turns in agony and despair to the Prophet.

> BAJA: Ah, villains, dare you touch my sacred arms?
> O Mahomet! O sleepy Mahomet!
> ZAB: O cursed Mahomet,' that mak'st us thus
> The slaves to Scythians rude and barbarous![25]

The episode in which Bajazeth is taken out of the cage to serve as a foot stool for Tamburlaine to ascend the throne is a grim illustration of imprinting on the outer world the stamp of sovereignty. Tamburlaine, it is announced in the beginning, sets out with a thirst to conquer the Eastern world and it is learnt that the territories are falling one by one to the attack to serve as material for him to display his power, victories come effortlessly. And if it is so, where then is the necessity of such a conduct of barbaric humiliation meted out to a monarch? There is hardly any justification of such a show of moral violence other than the one that it could be a codified ritual of the pagan world. Nevertheless, the philosophy that Tamburlaine opts out to espouse is of unbridled passion for individualism that has no moral sanction in the world of the civilized.

The Renaissance age might glorify Tamburlaine for the expansion of his individuality to the utmost but in Aristotelian sense he is not a great 'souled man' and his heroic image is deflated during the process to an "insolent and blood-thirsty tyrant" for want of moral commitment which humanism demands. The episode shows Tamburlaine standing on the back of Bajazeth. He invokes God as a witness to behold terror personified, unleashed on the fallen emperors,

> Now clear the triple region of the air,
> And let the Majesty of Heaven be hold
> Their scourage and terror tread on emperors,
> Smile, starts that reign'd at my nativity,
> And dim the brightness of their neighbour lamps;
> Disdain to borrow light of Cynthia![26]

which may look rather unpalatable today but because Tamburlaine is "a young man's vision: we may become immortal like the gods",[27] there seems to be little unconvincingness about it, if seen from the standpoint of the historical context of the time.

One wonders what God he is invoking as a witness to see him treading on the emperors in this fashion—the biblical God or a God of Scourage and terror he personifies. Bajazeth is not broken even in state of captivity, he is alive to the honour to self and sovereignty which is seen when, to Tamburlaine's asking "Bring out my stool", he pours curses on the tyrant and wishes him die of poison collected from the 'moorish fens'. This stirs the beast of ambition and wrath in Tamburlaine, much to the adversary's annoyance and rejection.

> TAMBUR: But, villain, thou that wishest this to me,
> Fall prostrate on the low disdainful earth,
> And be the footstool of great Tamburlaine,
> That I may rise into my royal throne.
> BAJA: First shalt thou rip my bowels with thy sword
> And sacrifice my heart to death and hell,
> Before I yield to such a slavery.[28]

And when Bajazeth is put again into the cage, he suddenly becomes conscious of his dignity and asks, "Is this a place for mighty Bajazeth?" But what is significant is that Bajazeth's god is not the Biblical God but a man turned into a tyrant god, the very personification of over-ambitiousness and pride. Tamburlaine hardly understands the significance of love of humanity. This finds expression in unambiguous terms:

> There, while he lives, shall Bajazeth be kept,
> And, where I go, be thus in triumph drawn;
> And thou, his wife, shall feed him with the scraps
> My servitors shall bring thee from my board.[29]

Tamburlaine begins to speak in third person and then switches over to the first. This shift from third person 'he' to first person I is symbolic of his self-styled drift from the average level of humanity to the distinct touch of individualism. The imagery and language are proper to the theme of the play and cater to the taste of the Elizabethans who were fond of such high astounding terms and phrases. Westlund has rightly pointed out that the rhetoric is closely related with the power quest: Tamburlaine's exaggerated statements of his own prowess become literally true during the course of the drama: "hyperbole becomes fact and rhetoric not only defines the central character but also determines the course of the play's action."[30]

The scene in which a banquet is laid, perhaps to create the impression of Tamburlaine's terror, verges on comicality and melodrama. It is a show of sadism—some are fed, some remaining unfed whereas for Tamburlaine it is a treat. When scraps of food are thrown to the royal captives in the cages, the dramatist's Muse turns contrary, cursing Tamburlaine.

> BAJA: Ye Furies, that can mask invisible,
> Drive to the bottom of Avernus' pool,
> And in your hands bring hellish poison up,
> And squeeze it in the cup of Tamburlaine!
> Or, winged snakes of Lerna, cast your stings,
> And leave your venoms in this tyrant's dish!
> ZAB: And may this banquet prove as ominous
> As Progne's to th' adulterous Thracian king
> That fed upon the substance of his child![31]

Bajazeth and Zabina refuse to feed on the thrown-away victuals. Despair sets in and they feel that perhaps the moral universe has turned upside down. The intensity of pangs of hunger and unimaginable humiliation has raised them to heroic stature. Zabina sees little hope of ending of their sufferings in a godless world wherein there is left

no Mahomet, no God,
No fiend, no fortune, nor no hope of end
To our infamous, monstrous slaveries.[32]

Bajazeth sends Zabina away to bring water for "my burning breast". Alone in the cage, he brains himself against the cage. On her re-entry what Zabina sees is horror. Zabina is the human image shaken by agony and shivering sensation of the dread of death. She utters curses on Tamburlaine in broken prose. "Tamburlaine, Tamburlaine! — Let the soldiers be buried. — Hell, death, Tamburlaine, hell! — Make ready my coach, my chair, my jewels. — I come, I come, I come, I come!"[33] And saying this, she strikes her head against the iron bars of the cage and destroys herself. The bloody spectacle raises Zabina and Bajazeth high in Zenocrate's eyes. They also command our pity. Their destruction is an act of martyrdom to the terror of history and to the Renaissance ideal. There is no parallel to this episode in history but this is what Marlowe's imagination could conceive of to reflect the spirit of the time. The thrice repeated line as Zenocrate speaks "Behold the Turk and his great empress", depicts her deep anguish but it is surely a stamp of their triumph which, she feels, is moral. Zenocrate seeks pardon of God for Tamburlaine's atrocities, heaped on man without even being aware of the slipperiness and futility of the worldly pomp and glory. Her words showing Tamburlaine fighting for "scepters and for slippery crowns" point to the vanity of human wishes.

Zenocrate is critical of Tamburlaine's world-view which is incompatible with the moral precepts of the Renaissance humanism. He remains a 'sphered', and "so mean a man" in her eyes for his 'lawless rapine' and plunder. She warns him that gods will not let his designs reach fruition and urges upon him to "pity my distressed plight". She asks for liberty for her people which shows that she shares the humanists' viewpoint who value human freedom most and are opposed to all authoritarian and totalitarian forces responsible for the dehumanization of man.

> The gods, defenders of the innocent,
> Will never prosper your intended drifts,
> That thus oppress poor friendless passengers.
> Therefore at least admit us liberty.[34]

Hers is the voice of an ethical humanist who "relies on the arts of intelligence to defend, enlarge and enhance the areas of human freedom in the world".[35]

Tamburlaine, as Marlowe projects, is more than what he speaks of himself as the Scourage of God. That is, he is not all a "monstrous as gorgon prince of hell" as Soldan describes, dreaming of war-glory. He uses sword as power-symbol toward which his Renaissance imagination is directed by the accounts of the English sailors and explorers on the land and the sea. What redeems the clang of the swords is his aliveness to beauty in nature and love of Zenocrate. Zenocrate is the poet's vision of an ideal beauty that casts a spell on the barbaric imagination of Tamburlaine which finds expression in fine poetic images,

> Zenocrate, lovelier that the love of Jove,
> Brighter than is the silver Rhodope,
> Fairer than whitest snow on Scythian hills,
> Thy person is more worth to Tamburlaine
> Than the possession of the Persian crown.[36]

The use of the two epithets 'fair' and 'divine' in the description of her beauty shows that his ideal is not earthly.

> Ah, fair Zenocrate! Divine Zenocrate!
> Fair is too foul an epithet for thee.[37]

The ideal of all Marlovian heroes is high but being unearthly it remains unrealized. Faustus admires the beauty of Helen's phantom knowing that it is not real but a spirit. Both Faustus and Tamburlaine are symbols of lasciviousness—they admire the physical charm but there is no human touch in it because they do not love their object of admiration.

It is after his victory over Bajazeth that Tamburlaine becomes more and more blood thirsty and aggressively merciless. Overwhelmed by Caesar-like conceit of power, he stands erect like a tower claiming to be "the chiefest lamp of all the earth". The projection of Tamburlaine as a superhuman being is no doubt the central argument of the play which is worked out by the alchemy of the poetic power, with full conviction and belief in human potentialities. After the overthrow of the Persians and the Turks, the Soldan of Egypt, Zenocrate's father, remains to confront Tamburlaine's colonial adventure. The Soldan gives a clarion call to the slumbering Egyptians to rise to the occasion to meet 'the rogue of Volga', who has held his daughter, Zenocrate as his concubine. The Soldan seems to set his heart to avenge Zenocrate's dishonour.

> Were all the world conspir'd to fight for him,
> Nay, were he devil, as he is no man,
> Yet in revenge of fair Zenocrate,
> Whom he detaineth in despite of us,
> This arm should send him down to Erebus,
> To shroud his shame in darkness of the night.[38]

The device of symbolism is employed in the use of the colour-pattern to suggest the humorous temper of Tamburlaine. The colour of the tents on the first day was white which on the second day was changed to red. On the 'third day when the scene opens, the tents have the 'cruel'st hue' which is 'black' portending death to all, irrespective of "sex, degree and age".

> His coal-black colours, everywhere advanc'd,
> Threaten our city with a general spoil;[39]

The Governor of Damascus is of the view that the virgins be sent to Tamburlaine to seek clemency because war would mean a wilful overthrow. The proposal of peace is a genuine gesture of goodwill and humility but it is too late. He greets the virgins who approach him pleading for mercy with derisive cry,

"What, are the turtles frayed out of their nests". He feels pity but swears destruction for their failure to see the fluttering of the white flags earlier, suggesting mercy and forgiveness.

> Alas, poor fools, must you be first shall feel
> The sworn destruction of Damascus?
> They knew my custom; could they not as well
> Have sent ye out when first my milk-white flags,
> Through which sweet Mercy threw her gentle beams,
> Reflexed them on your disdainful eyes
> As now when fury and incensed hate
> Flings slaughtering terror from my coal-black tents,
> And tells for truth submissions comes too late?[40]

The sight of the virgins evokes pity but it is compulsion and craziness for power that renders it sterile as the word 'Alas!' suggests. It is the sword power that makes Tamburlaine a "sacred emperor", in their eyes. However, the virgins are put to death which suggests that Tamburlaine is transformed into a monster. One wonders what virtue-god Tamburlaine worships and what morality he adheres to. M.C. Bradbrook has rightly pointed out that "Tamburlaine's ambition has no definite object, it exists in and for itself".[41] And thus it is nothing unusual if he shows disrespect to the kings who are weak to defend the crown which, in Elizabethan age, was a metaphor of all 'desirable ends'.

The play reaches its climax in his conquests of the Soldan of Egypt and the crowning of his daughter, Zenocrate as the Empress of the kingdoms he has conquered. The marriage preparations are underway but within the existing framework of the plot the action can hardly be termed as tragic. The tragic issues from the sufferings of those who are destroyed while opposing Tamburlaine's imperialistic designs and love of violence. The truth of it becomes articulate in Menaphon.

> Thirsting with sovereignty and love of arms,
> His lofty brows in folds do figure death,[42]

Marlowe's humanism is reflected in the portrayal of Tamburlaine's enemies in the line of Machiavelli and other humanists who describe what men do, rather than what they ought to do. He shows them as much the victim of power and gold as he but it is the superhuman urge in him by virtue of which he wields fortunes on his side to tower over them in dignity, power and beauty of speech. It is they who also have partly deified him by using images which hardly fit into the scale of the human. For example, Tamburlaine is frequently equated with god or a devil as a part of the theatrical device even by those who oppose him to create terror which he himself claims to be of its extension.

And thus ends the First Part of the play in triumph and glory, showing Tamburlaine, as his dying words tell, as much a man as we all are suffering from human frailties and imperfections. It is by virtue of being a man of more a state of heightened consciousness that he aims at aspiring high but where it takes him to in absence of the proper understanding of self in relation to God and universe is what the book dramatizes and which is its strength.

NOTES

1. The central theme of the First book of Lucan is the march of Caesar in 49 BC from Gaul toward Rome. It takes in its sweep the part of the territories which fourteen centuries later were to be the scene of Tamburlaine's exploits (Frederick S. Boas, p. 74).
2. Frederick S. Boas, *Christopher Marthlow: A Biographical and Critical Studies*, Oxford: The Clarenden Press, 1940, p. 76.
3. *Shakespeare and the Predecessors*, p. 33.
4. *Tamburlaine Part First*, in *Christopher Marlowe: The Complete Plays*, J.B. Steane (ed.), London: Penguin Books Ltd., 1969, p. 105.
5. *Ibid.*, p. 112.
6. *Ibid.*, p. 105.
7. *Ibid.*, pp. 105-06.
8. *Ibid.*, p. 106.

9. *Idem.*
10. *Ibid.*, p. 107.
11. *Idem.*
12. Frederick. S Boas sees Marlowe's source of Zenocrate in Virgil. Zenocrate is Virgil's Lavinia, the daughter of King Latinus who was already bethrothed to Turnus, King of Ratilia. Turnus turned against Aeneas whom Virgil makes win Lavinia when he comes to Italy in the later part of the epic. Similarly, Zenocrate has been bethrothed to the King of Arabia, who fights Tamburlaine in the last scene of Part One for his country and love.
13. *Tamburlaine*, Part One, p. 113.
14. *Ibid.*, p. 112.
15. *Idem.*
16. J.P. Van Prag, "What is Humanism", in The Humanist Alternative: Some Definitions of Humanism, *op. cit.*, p. 45.
17. *Tamburlaine,* Part One, *op. cit.*, p. 116.
18. *Ibid.*, p. 117.
19. *Ibid.*, p. 120.
20. *Ibid.*, pp. 132-33.
21. *Ibid.*, p. 134.
22. *Ibid.*, p. 135.
23. *Ibid.*, p. 142.
24. *Tamburlaine*, *The Great*, Part Two, p. 257.
25. *Ibid.*, p. 149.
26. *Ibid.*, pp. 152-53.
27. U. Ellis Fermor, *Christopher Marlowe*, Metheun, London, 1927.
28. *Tamburlaine,* Part One, *op. cit.*, p. 152.
29. *Ibid.*, p. 154.
30. Westlund, "The Orthodox Christian Framework of Marlowe's *Faustus*: Studies in English Literature, 1500-1900", Vol. II, No. 2, Spring, 1963, p. 192.
31. *Tamburlaine*, Part One, *op. cit.*, p. 158.
32. *Ibid.*, p. 170.
33. *Ibid.*, p. 172.

34. *Ibid.*, p. 113.
35. Sydney Hook, "The Snare of Definitions," in *The Humanist Alternative: Some Definitions of Humanism*, *op. cit.*, p. 34.
36. *Tamburlaine*, Part One, *op. cit.*, p. 114.
37. *Ibid.*, p. 166.
38. *Ibid.*, pp. 150-51.
39. *Ibid.*, p. 162.
40. *Ibid.*, p. 164.
41. M.C. Bradbrook, *Themes and Conventions in Elizabethan Tragedy*, Cambridge University Press, 1969, p. 138.
42. *Tamburlaine*, Part One, *op. cit.*, p. 120.

3

Tamburlaine Part Second

The trend, as set forth in Part One, continues in Part Second also: how the flimsy philosophy of self-reliance as generated by false humanism is destined to final failure. The loss of the spiritual centre of the Being involves the loss of self at the same time and thus where at the end this miscalculation of self leads man to is a point of interest. The truth is that Tamburlaine "swings rapidly from his assertion of man's greatness, independent of God, to the other blasphemy of denying human greatness altogether" which results in the shrinkage of both body and spirit.

Marlowe wrote the Second Part of *Tamburlaine, The Great* as the Prologue heralds, after its First Part received 'the general welcome' of the public. The implicit cause of popularity was the immediacy of the choice of the theme outside the 'native salt'. The First Part is a glorification of human will, the Second Part shows something different: man's desires and aspirations may be limitless but their fulfillment is limited by forces outside man's control, death being one that

> cuts off the progress of his pump.
> And murderous Fate throw all his triumphs down.[1]

However, what constitutes the unity of the two parts is the continuing theme of war and the predicament of an aspiring soul. The major episodes, spreading over 21 scenes (Part One comprises 18 scenes) which the play, the Prologue tells, dramatizes, deal with Tamburlaine's impassionate war-fury, the death of Zenocrate and the exhortation and discipline to initiate the three sons into the skill of fighting, including the

The Callapine's escape episode serves twofold purpose; first, that the symptoms of betrayal and feebleness have begun to appear in Tamburlaine's empire because no enemy of his ever escaped alive in this manner and no officer, as Clifford Leech points out, turned ever so corrupt and corrupting. Second, Marlowe keeps the crown motif at the centre of the episode in his study of man in relation to time's disorders that Goethe later aimed at projecting in *Faust*: falling an easy prey to gold and sensuality. The words of Callapine's keeper, Almeda, "Shall I be made a king for my labour?" are a fine burlesque of the power quest associated with the crown. It is a parallel to what Theridamas and Usumcasane discuss in Part One to humour Tamburlaine and partly to give vent to their own aspirations of becoming a king.

USUM: To be a king is half to be a god

THERID: A: A god is not so glorious as a king.[5]

Callapine's seduction of Almeda shows a brilliant insight into the mechanism of human mind in a given situation. Callapine betrays no traits of weakness of passion. He is noble, shrewd and has the gift of brilliant eloquence that has the orphic charm to hypnotize man Marlowe creates in Tamburlaine. His promises centring around the kingly glory are hard to resist. He tells Almeda that a Turkish boat of royal fleet is anchored to the river side, waiting any time for his release. It will take the two safe to Turkish seas stretching between the islands of Cyprus and Crete and thus that involves no risk. What Callapine, who is born to be the monarch of the western world, says in not a false he plays on Almeda's head, but truth. When they reach Turky, they will be accorded a royal welcome. Almeda will see

a hundred kings and more,

Upon their knees, all bid me welcome home.

Amongst so many crowns of burnish'd gold.

And he will be free to choose any crown of his liking. Besides, he will own a thousand galleys draughted with gold and manned by Christian slaves and

> The Grecian virgins shall attend on thee,
> Skilful in music and in amorous lays,
> As fair as was Pygmalion's ivory girl.[6]

Besides, Almeda will ride in triumph through the streets, the chariot being drawn by naked Negroes on pavements covered with Turkey carpets. The procession will be led by a hundred bassoes "Clothed in crimson silk" on Barbarian steeds. It is not that Almeda is a caricature of Renaissance lust of power, pomp and glory but what is true is that such a glorious and princely offer can easily make any one's imagination run riot. That is why it has the desired effect on Almeda. He shows sign of falling in the line: "If I should let you go, would you be as good as your word?" Callapine swears by the hand of Mahomet to make him a king and his mate. He acts courageously and takes it a sovereign duty on himself "to revenge my father's death". And thus with the help of enemy's man he slips away from the prison to fulfil the task.

And it is after the dramatization of the two important events—the treaty between the Turks and the Christians and Callapine's escape that Tamburlaine appears. The time gap is used as a device of suspension to create the illusion of greatness. We are waiting breathlessly for Tamburlaine's appearance since it is his play. The action gains momentum and shows departure. Tamburlaine has control over more than half the geographical world but the signs of weariness, as felt by Zenocrate because of the continuing clanging of swords and the problems of the three sons who wear amorous rather than martial looks, are the obstacles outside the enemy's might which he has to surmount. He finds them "too dainty for war", their fingers play on a flute rather than holding a sword. He thinks that they are "bastards, not my sons". But when Zenocrate speaks high of the youngest son, Celebinus, he claims him to be his son and feeling assured of his valiancy asks him to rise to his expectation and be the scourge and terror of the world otherwise "you are not sons of Tamburlaine". What a fancy to measure the piety of the umbilical ties!

CELEBI: Yes father you shall see me
If I live, have under me as many kinds as you,
And march with such a multitude of men
As all the world shall tremble at their view.
TAMBUR: These words assure me, boy, thou art my son.
When I am old and cannot manage arms
Be thou the scourge and terror of the world.[7]

The imagery has the taint of the macabre which Marlowe employs to suggest the sinister nature of Tambularine's dreamy conquests. Tamburlaine's empire is metaphorically likened with a 'chair' floating in a sea of blood but Celebrinus tells his mother that he is prepared to sail to it.

For, if his chair were in a sea of blood,
I would prepare a ship and sail to it.
Ere I would lose the title of a king.[8]

It is the lust of power and wealth that transforms the valiant Turks and the Christians into demons of Machiavellian opportunism which is visible in the breach of the treaty between them and the resultant fight in which Sigismund dies and the victorious Turks retire to celebrate their happy conquest. What does the tearing of the solemn article of peace into pieces suggest, which the two confirmed—Sigismund by Christ and Orcanes by Mahomet, outside man's turning untrue to each other which is in contravention with the spirit of humanism? The Turks and the Christians should have fought united against the enemy, but their hostilities and distrust make Tamburlaine's conquests less challenging.

Tamburlaine plays a relatively passive part in Part Two in comparison to the role played in earlier scenes of Part One but his temper remains unchanged. This is seen in the answer he gives to Zenocrate's question, "When wilt thou leave these arms?", that he would cease fighting when the great upheaval in nature takes place the probability of which is all illusion.

When heaven shall cease to move on both the poles,
And when the ground, whereon my soldiers march,

Shall rise aloft and touch the horned moon,
And not before, my sweet Zenocrate.[9]

The closing scene in which Zenocrate is dying is eventful which makes a mockery of Tamburlaine's boast of holding Fates in his hands. The superman in him is left pining for her. The opening dialogue running for 37 lines is a sort of panegyric on Zenocrate who in his eyes is not earthly reality. Even in moments of sorrow the utterance is not human, he sees in a vision Zenocrate's entry into heaven, and bids the angles to entertain her.

Now walk the angles on the walls of heaven,
As sentinels to warn th' immortal souls
To entertain divine Zenocrate:[10]

The five-time repetition of the line as an invocation to Zenocrate, "To entertain the divine Zenocrate" is an expression of the romantic impulse ever yearning after unrealized ideal of perfection. That is why its appeal, as Boas points out, is more to imagination rather than to heart. Tamburlaine breaks down and expresses a wish to die with the Queen which presents a contrasting image of his earlier self. The death of Zenocrate leaves him "raving, impatient, desperate and mad". The poetry accommodates the emotional fury, born of, as he feels, god's usurption of Zenocrate.

What, is she dead? Techelles, draw thy sword,
And wound the earth, that it may cleave in twain,
And we descend into th' infernal vaults,
To hale the Fatal Sisters by the hair,
And throw them in the triple moat of hell,
For taking hence my fair Zenocrate.[11]

The amorous Jove, he says, has snatched away his love. His response to Zenocrate's death is of violence which is an intrinsic element of his nature. In sheer desperation and hopelessness he turns abruptly to his pillars of strength, Theridamas and Usumcasane and asks them to take up arms against gods and

break the frame of heaven;
Batter the shining place of the sun,
And shiver all the starry firmament.[12]

He urges Zenocrate also to pity him and come down from heaven to live with him again. Theridamas consoles him and makes an appeal to bear the separation patiently.

Ah, good my lord, be patient! She is dead,
And all this raging cannot make her live,
If words might serve, our voice hath rent the air;
If tears, our eyes have water'd all the earth;
If grief, our murder'd hearts have strained forth blood.
Nothing prevails, for she is dead, my lord.[13]

The words "for she is dead" pierce Tamburlaine heart. As explained by Theridamus, he takes her death a finality to her earthly existence yet he somehow develops an illusion that perhaps she still lives. He orders her body to be embalmed and wrapped in a sheet of gold till he dies and then they both together will be interr'd in a rich mausoleum.

And, till I die, thou shalt not be interr'd
Then in as rich a tomb as Mausolus'
We both will rest, and have one epitaph
Writ in as many several languages
As I have conquer'd kingdoms with my sword.[14]

The vision of holding the Fates in hand disappears. The idea to confer immortality on Zenocrate is frustrated because this time the fight is with nature, man's mortality which is hard to surmount. It is tragic irony that Tamburlaine, despite having a vast stretch of empire and military strength and the power of rhetoric, will not be able to save Zenocrate or prolong her life. The tragic hero at the end gains illumination which is one requirement of tragedy and which brings man closer to vision. Tamburlaine gains no such recognition and if there is any, it is at the level of the audience who accept death as a reality and an extension of life on earth. Thus, Tamburlaine's failure to develop a cogent view of reality even in moments of crisis portends similar fate befalling him.

The hearse of Zenocrate is being borne by four attendants, a doleful march is sounded and the town that saw her die is in flames. Is that what Tamburlaine meant by being the "scourage of God and terror to the world"? Will the wreckless destruction of the town, symbolic of human creation, be of any worth in the realization of his goal? Or will the world honour his command, not to stirring the debris for human habitation? He desires the scene of destruction to remain a mausoleum to commemorate his love for Zenocrate which ironically shows that it is hardly a case of admiration of the object of love. A pillar is raised in her memory with the inscription written on it in three languages—Arabian, Hebrew, Greek:

> 'This town, being burnt by Tamburlaine the Great,
> Forbids the world to build it up again'.[15]

What a noble creature Tamburlaine is!

Many years are passed since Tamburlaine's exploits in Part One. The three sons, Calyphas, Amyras, Celebinus, are advancing to military age. And since they seem to be less enthusiastic about war Tamburlaine is much worried about their future. Thus, it is nothing surprising if he abruptly turns to give them a lecture on the rudiments of war, particularly the method of carrying a besieged city to assault. The warfare schooling must have been an interesting exercise for the Elizabethans, partly because they developed fondness for sports and partly because they were exposed to the constant threats of Spanish power.

Marlowe, in order to frustrate Tamburlaine's hopes that his sons would follow his example, paints the eldest Calyphas different from his two brothers. Calyphas is a foil to Callapine, who made an escape from Tamburlaine's captivity by bribing the keeper. After Sigismund's defeat, Callapine joins Orcanes and is crowned as the emperor of the tributary kings who have gathered to oppose the Scythian's' advance. The two armies come face to face and Marlowe again romanticizes

Tamburlaine's stature to the level of the Greek heroes when he cries at the Turkish force.

Ye petty kings of Turkey, I am come,
As Hector did into the Grecian camp,
To overdare the pride of Graecia,
And set his warlike person to the view
Of fierce Achilles, rival of his fame.
I do you honour in the simile;
For, if I should, as Hector did Achilles,
The worthiest knight that ever brandish'd sword,
Challenge in combat any of you all,
I see how fearfully ye would refuse,
And fly my glove as from as scorpion.[16]

The alarms of fight are heard off the stage but what is significant is Calyphas's lingering in his tent despite the urges of his brothers to come out and fight war. What he speaks in return shows that either the spirit of Tamburlaine is less dominant in him or perhaps he has developed an anti-romantic attitude to war and like a Shavian hero is interested more in the value of preservation of life somehow on the battle field rather than ceasing to exist. Conscience keeps pricking him to be human and not a blood thirsty demon.

I know, sir, what it is to kill a man;
It works remorse of conscience in me.
I take no pleasure to be murderous,
No care for blood when wine will quench my thirst.[17]

Tamburlaine has seen how the 'red' colour (of blood) stirs heroism in man and thus he uses psychology to extenuate the fear associated with blood-shedding from Calyphas's mind. He cuts his arm to give a further lesson in the art of soldiering[18] saying

A wound is nothing, be it ne'er so deep;
Blood is the god of war's rich livery.[19]

He proceeds like a psychiatrist to cure the crippleness of the soul, not of the body. He asks his sons to wash their hands with blood so as to be a fit follower of great Tamburlaine, but for Calyphas, the sight is 'pitiful'. The flow of blood is sinister because it foreshadows a terrible event to follow which is his own death. This state of passivity and aversion to war cannot save Calyphas from Tamburlaine's wrath. After Tamburlaine returns victorious, he stabs Calyphas to death, invoking Jove to receive one whose deeds do not suit the philosophy of a Scythian camp:

> Here, Jove, receive his fainting soul again,
> A form not meet to give that subject essence
> Whose matter is the flesh of Tamburlaine,
> Wherein an incorporeal spirit moves,
> Made of the mould whereof thyself consists,
> Which makes me valiant, proud, ambitious.[20]

Tamburlaine's act is not in accord with the spirit of the ethical humanism which lays emphasis "on right relations between people as the most important thing". Earlier such scenes of crude horror and violence were enacted off the stage. And if any violence was indispensable it was used when the dramatist wanted to say something significant which otherwise was not possible to say so.

If humanism is bound up with its existential value, then certainly Calyphas is a positive demonstration of the humanist morality which "is based on the acknowledgement of the mutual solidarity of men", opposed to self-interest as practiced by Tamburlaine. It is in this sense that Tamburlaine represents false humanism opposed to the true humanism which is embodied in Calyphas. Calyphas is not averse to war but he does not look upon war-like Tamburlaine as romantic glorification of human valour or the sole means of expansion of self. War is a senseless activity, a metaphor of human suffering, he knows, and that is why his protest against and defiance of Tamburlainean war-hysteria is a powerful denunciation of the demon of power lust in man. Tamburlaine in self-glorification draws heavily upon the classical gods but his attitude towards them is ambivalent which is characteristic of the age itself. On the one hand, he is grateful to Jove for creating in him "a great enemy that the mountain-hurling Titans" he proclaims himself, "arch monarch of the world/ Crowned and invested by the hand of Jove". But on the other, he denounces Jupiter in the same breath for sending "to my issue such a soul created of the massy dregs of earth". The earth-imagery, he employs to denounce Calyphas in spirit, not in body, is interesting that finds its echo in Prospero's condemnation of Caliban also as 'earth-earthy' when he claimed the lawful heritage of the island. Prospero is the god of imperialism and so is Tamburlaine in whom the Elizabethan audience saw the expansion of their own aspiration for a vast empire over the lands and the seas. But his logic is absurd that it is ignominy to have a son who will not fight as if belligerency or the philosophy of violence is the sole test of one's humanity.

Marlowe repeats the barbaric inhuman episode of Part One wherein Bajazeth is carried about in a cage and used as a footstool in Part Two. This time the pageant is spun around the captive kings who are drawing Tamburlaine's chariot which is Marlowe's own invention. Babylon is the last exploit of Tamburlaine and, as per planning, from thence he would reach his native city of Samarcand in triumphal procession. But the mode of transportation he chooses is utterly monstrous, the chariot is being driven by the conquered kings. His rebuke to these 'human steeds',

> Holla, ye pampered jades of Asia!
>
> What, can ye draw but twenty miles a day.[21]

has become 'an off-quoted parody' of show of power in Elizabethan literature. This grotesque show of human supremacy inflates his egotism. The fancy takes flights and he becomes oblivious of human identity to the extent that he compares his drive with Jove's course through the sky.

> Then in my coach, like Saturn's royal son
>
> Mounted his shining chariot gilt with fire,
>
> And drawn with princely eagles through the path
>
> Pav'd with bright crystal and enchas'd with stars

When all the gods stand gazing at his pomp,
So will I ride through Samarcanda strets,
Until my soul, dissever'd from this flesh,
Shall mount the milk-white way, and meet him there.[22]

With the fall of Babylon, the savage in Tamburlaine becomes more and more aggressive. The Governor of Babylon is captured and when Tamburlaine orders to hang him up in chains on the walls of the city he offers him the treasure of gold which he had hidden "under a hollow bank in the lake to save his life. But it is a pity that the 'baiting of gold', which is used as a warfare tactics in such cases, is perhaps inadequate to gratify the hunger of the god of Imperialism and thus the Governor is shot dead at his command. The action becomes more melodramatic. Tamburlaine embodies the very spirit of the two great Elizabethan movements, travel and colonization. His ride on the back of the conquered kings is a part of process of dispossession and enslavement of the native population that began with the sailors who went out to explore the universe and brought home the dispossessed slaves, they called them 'wondrous trophies'.[23] He orders Techelles to drown all men, women and children in the lake and leave no Babylonian alive in the town. Such an inhuman and barbaric show of power makes us feel as if he has virtually replaced the divine machinery to crush man at will. The Turkish Alcoran is also burnt by his orders. Christianity was also disgraced by the falsifiers of faith when they broke the treaty with the Turks which they swore by the name of Christ. Tamburlaine seems to be the agent of a God he himself defines. It is certainly not the traditional God, all-loving and benevolent, but a God of thunder and lighting, full of revenge and fury. And to him he will obey.

There is a God, full of revenging wrath,
From whom the thunder and the lightning breaks,
Whose scourage I am, and him will I obey.[24]

In defying Mahomet his departure from all conventional religious observances is complete. It is at the acme of power that the warrior in Tamburlaine is struck down by nature which is suggested by a fine conceit of the waning moon used by Callapine to moralise that those who rise must have a fall.

> Yet, when the pride of Cynthia is at full,
> She wanes again; and so shall his, I hope;[25]

Callapine is realistic about his own might as measured out against Tamburlaine's. As a matter of truth what had made Tamburlaine greater is not the force but 'fortunes' and 'victories'. Marlowe has created such an extraordinary hypnotizing spell of personality in him that his very looks would put the Turkish armies put to flight.

> My looks shall make them fly; and, might I follow,
> There should not one of all the villain's power
> Live to give offer of another fight.[26]

Tamburlaine talks of hastening to Persia 'after all over victories' which perhaps shows the end of his exploits. When a messenger appears announcing Callapine's attack on his army it is sufficient to re-energize his dying spirits. He takes it a celestial dose that Jove has sent from above "to recure my pain". The last victory against the Turkish forces is a sort of prelude to his death. He abruptly asks his soldiers to stay because he feels 'distempered'. He is stricken with sickness which he fears would prove him to be a man whereas in the last moments of his life he wishes to uphold the image of a god, as one who remains unaffected by any human frailty. As Faustus is unwilling to remain "but Faustus and a man", so Tamburlaine does not want to remain a man to be assaulted by sickness.

> Shall sickness prove me now to be a man,
> That have been term'd the terror of the world?

A dreamy vision spun around vain fantasies of godhood!

Thinking that it is not some earthly but heavenly powers who, being envious of his health, are afflicting his soul, he questions their identity.

> What daring god torments my body thus,
> And seeks to conquer mightly Tamburlaine?

The nightmare of being the 'Scourge of God' continues and Tamburlaine totally becomes oblivious of human reality in his protestations of fighting out gods. He asks Techelles and others to draw swords to wage war against heaven without being aware of its ironic implications that nature has its own laws to follow. Tamburlaine's powers are flagging but Marlowe's poetic Muse remains intact to create the illusion of omnipotence. Contrary to the medieval belief—gods striking men—Tamburlaine's answer that is it is men marching to strike gods at once makes him, to quote Boas "a veritable incarnation of the genius of the Renaissance".

> Come, let us march against the powers of heaven,
> And set black streamers in the firmament,
> To signify the slaughter of the gods.[27]

As Tamburlaine is nearing death, the imagery tends to be more of moral violence and dissolution. The physicians prepare a potion for him to drink which, it is hoped, will "abate the fury of your fit". Techelles calls the malady too violent to last which brings Tamburlaine to the ultimate realization for the first time that he is mortal and one who lives has to die. "Not last, Techelles! No, for I shall die". He sees a phantom of death and calls it 'my slave'. When he was at the height of his martial glory, death no doubt once waited on the edge of his sword. The victim of his wrath was killed the moment he wished it so. In other words, he himself was the agency of death. But what happens to the image of self-anointed emissary of destiny when he is nearing death? He becomes aware of mortality, "for I shall die". But the manner in which he describes death is the force of poetry, not of his human strength. He calls it 'my slave' who, as he imagines, flies away at his glances but the truth is that 'Shaking and quivering' are not of death but of his infirmity, signifying dissipation of Tamburlainism the play is built upon

> See, where my slave, the ugly monster Death,
> Shaking and quivering, pale and wan for fear,
> Stands aiming at me with his murdering dart,

Who flies away at every glance I give,
And, when I look away, comes stealing on![28]

He has lost the power of seeing, the blindness is spiritual. The appearance and disappearance of death "Look, where he goes! But, see, he comes again" is all hallucination. A map is spread before him wherein he traces those places which he has conquered, and those that are left still unconquered for his sons to conquer. This includes the project of cutting of Suez Canal; which was a part of his exploits.

Whereas the Terrene and the Red Sea meet,
Being distant less than full a hundred leadgues,
I meant to cut a channel to them both,
That men might quickly sail to India.[29]

But it is a fond hope that he leaves the construction work for his two sons to accomplish and fulfill his ambitions left unfulfilled to live immortally.

My flesh, divided in your precious shapes,
Shall still retain my spirit, though I die,
And live in all your seeds immortally.[30]

What is now left for the dying Scythian warrior is parting with the crown. The followers, as he wills, assist him to descend from the chariot. The episode of power-transference must have been painful for those who are drugged by the delusions of omnipotence but it is a historical necessity which is to be accepted as it is. For Theridamas, the change of crown is a 'woeful change'. Amyras is crowned as the king. The occasion is very solemn and eventful but what mars its graveness is Tamburlaine's education to the sons which has the taint of savagery and violence.

He bids farewell to his sons and followers and dies with the words.

For Tamburlaine, the Scourge of God, must die.[31]

The words 'The Scourge of God' are written on the little page also which keep reverberating a number of time like minute's gun as a threat to the world he sets out to conquer.

But what happens at the end? Could he ever become 'the Scourge of God'? Agreed that in the historical context, the story is a success story in a technical sense which embodies the very spirit of the age of exploration and colonization beyond the Atlantic. But for want of proper understanding of self in relation to society, God and the universe the odyssey at the end leaves the impression of waste and shows man as he is in face of nature. Second, Tamburlaine can hardly be accepted as a tragic character, fully in Aristotelian sense. Tragedy by definition is a story of extreme suffering of one or at the most of the two characters, conducting the hero at the end to death. Butcher says that it "satisfies a universal human need"[32] and moves in the realm of the spiritual. There is hardly any scene depicting Tamburlaine's agony born of the combat within the self which is a core ingredient in a tragedy.

The dominions raising arms against him are falling one by one, beginning with the fall of Persia to the defeat of the Soldan of Egypt and leaving Tamburlaine unhurt and unwounded. Nor do we find him in a 'to be or not to be' situation, confronting the crisis of existence. Unlike an Aristotelian hero for whom the moral goodness is a central virtue leading to happiness, he commits acts of savagery which hardly wins our imaginative sympathy. The ambition with which he sets out is anti-humanist. Humanism in the modern sense "is a concept of man focused upon a programme for humanity"[33] and Tamburlaine is unaware of the irony that the idea to be a 'terror' to the world rather than being a meaningful cog in human programme will displume him of honour and glory and destroy the human in him. His fall does not evoke pity. Nowhere is he seen as a victim of undeserved suffering or a case of more sin against than sinning as Lear is. But we certainly fear the Tamburlaine in us a victim of over-ambitiousness and desire for limitless power which even gods could not resist, what to say of men. "Desire of power", says Dryden, for its genesis in heaven, is noble but in men on earth becomes pernicious "a vicious seed"[34] in the possessor when he oversteps limitations. This implicit irony makes the play a common man tragedy.

NOTES

1. *Tamburlaine, the Great*, Part Two, p. 183.
2. Helen Gardener, "The Second Part of Tamburlaine the Great", in *Modern Language Review*, Vol. XXXVII, 1942.
3. *Tamburlaine, the Great*, Part Two, p. 185.
4. *Ibid.*, p. 187.
5. *Tamburlaine*, Part One, p. 129.
6. *Tamburlaine*, Part Two, p. 159.
7. *Ibid.*, pp. 192-93.
8. *Ibid.*, p. 193.
9. *Ibid.*, p. 191.
10. *Ibid.*, p. 204.
11. *Ibid.*, pp. 206-07.
12. *Ibid.*, p. 207.
13. *Idem.*
14. *Ibid.*, p. 208.
15. *Ibid.*, p. 211.
16. *Ibid.*, pp. 222-23.
17. *Ibid.*, p. 227.
18. For the lectures on warfare tactics and particularly the methods of carrying a besieged city by assault, Marlowe owes to Paul Ive's *Practise of Fortification* (F. Boas, p. 93).
19. *Ibid.*, p. 214.
20. *Ibid.*, p. 229.
21. *Ibid.*, p. 236.
22. *Ibid.*, pp. 239-40.
23. A.W. Verity (ed.) *The Tempest* "Introduction", London: Cambridge University Press, 1954, p. xxviii.

    In the wake of the two great Elizabethan movements—travel and colonization, the English sailors had been exploring the universe. Companies like the Virginia were formed and expeditions were sent out to plant settlement in far lands. The innumerable narratives of expeditions and descriptions of these unknown countries were printed. Prominent among them are Jourdain's *Discovery of the Barmudas*, Eden's *History of Travel* and Walter Raleigh's *Discovery of Guiana*. The sailors brought home the natives, the 'Indians', "monsters", they called them "wonderous trophies" and strange tales of their adventures.

24. *Ibid.*, p. 246.
25. *Tamburlaine, the Great*, Part Two, p. 249.
26. *Ibid.*, p. 253.
27. *Ibid.*, p. 251.
28. *Idem.*
29. *Ibid.*, pp. 253-54.
30. *Ibid.*, p. 255.
31. *Ibid.*, p. 257.
32. S.H. Butcher, (trans.) *Aristotle's Theory of Poetry and Fine Arts*, New Delhi: Kalyani Publishers, 1991, p. 272.
33. H.J. Blackham, "A Definition of Humanism" in *The Humanist Alternative: Some Definitions of Humanism*, *op. cit.* p. 37.
34. *Absalom and Achitophel* (lines 305-06).

4

Doctor Faustus

As Tamburlaine ends, so does Faustus as a victim of what Bardyaev calls the self-destructive principle in humanism. The play convincingly debunks the much-fancied benefits of self discovery in post-Renaissance theology that human nature, when cut off from its deepest foundations, as the votaries of anthropocentric humanism advocate, can attain self-reliance. If humanism freed man from the medieval world order and put him along the road of experimentation to understand the world on his own terms, it also robbed him of self-esteem when a free play of reason and creative will misled him to look upon himself as the very center of the universe rather than continuing to living with the idea that he is a reflection of the Divine Being. The Renaissance is the age of startling discoveries but it is also the discovery of the moral truths that man's moving away from the center to the periphery will not bring emancipation but impoverishment. Jacques Maritain terms this upheaval in human thought the tragedy of God which is closely related with the tragedy of man in the sense that in a bid to overcome 'authenticity', in the existential sense—to be what he is not—he turned indifferent to the divine idea of transcendence and reached a point the gravity of which finds utterance in what Nietzsche adds "Man is a shame and a disgrace and should be transcended".

Paul Oskar Kristeller says that whereas Aristotle was treated in isolation by the medieval scholastics, in Renaissance he was "read and interpreted in close conjunction with other Greek philosophers and writers" and was a preferred subject of discussion. Translations and summaries were made of his writings (Leonardo Bruni translated his *Ethics*, *Politics*, *Economics*). As a result of this wide interest in his ethical writings, "practically every writer of the period was acquainted with the main doctrines of Aristotle's ethics and was inclined to adopt them and to discuss them". Marlowe may not have been directly influenced by Aristotle in fashioning his heroes but certainly the influence is marked on what they try to attain: "the subjective aim of self expansion if equated with the objective ideal of Aristotelian greatness".[1] This is seen in Aristotle's concept of the Magnificent Man who has two things: he is resolute in his pursuit of greatness and second, he tolerates no rival in his sphere of influence. So does Faustus' rivalry stretch beyond God to be in the very state of godhood. And this makes the play a study in the fall of an intellectual turned-atheist when intellect is put to disuse. Marlowe's interest lies in projecting how man abuses his virtue and is destroyed during the process which is substantiated by what he states in the Prologue and the Epilogue.

In humanism, the emphasis is on free thought and atheism for its 'free thinking' is linked with humanism. But there is a line dividing the two categories: the humanists for their scientific world-outlook can be atheists, but all atheists are not humanists in the sense that the tendency of free thinking, might degenerate into licentiousness and moral violence. Later in the 19th century, Goethe took up the Faust-theme which persistently haunted his mind "practically the whole of his working life".[2] The theme of the expansion of self to the utmost bounds of the Infinite had a great appeal to the Renaissance mind. Man's wilful surrender to evil gives sensation of awe and fright yet it has its own fascination. Ignorance was condemned as a sin and man developed an inordinate passion for knowledge to know the world, contrary to the view of the idealists that the world is not knowable, it can be known only by supernatural powers. Faustus cuts short and gains this power by virtue of the pact with the devil and suffers, ironically speaking, moral decline and thus the dream of sounding, "the depth of that thou wilt profess" and be a divine in show" ends in sound and fury signifying nothing.

What happens thereafter raises a question; what Faustus makes of himself, whether man can rise to a level of awareness of the values which are within human control? Faustus is alive to the value of the individual judgement which, by implication, can be both positivistic and negativistic. Marlowe does not impose any pattern of value of his own, he leaves the audience free to judge Faustus's failure or success as they see it. However, the project is profoundly meaningful and illuminating which makes the audience at least to know "where the light is" and what is the morality of act and choice for the quester of reality in the existential sense. The poet says in *Hamlet*, "Our thoughts are ours, their ends none of our own". There is something that works through men and makes them instruments of a design which is not their own. The end is divorced from thought and man is left clashing on a 'darkling plain' in a bid to make sense of the senseless. This is the tragic paradox which puts the heroic in man to test.

A.C. Bradley rightly points out that the "tragic world is a world of action and action is the translation of thought into reality. Men and women strike into the existing order of things in pursuance of their ideas. But what they achieve is not what they intended, it is terribly unlike it".[3] Tamburlaine mocks at the idea of the power which they say, operates through men and sees nothing beyond human grasp. Faustus is the extension of that Tamburlainean indomitable will and unbridled passion for individualistic values and thus for the satisfaction of the spiritual nature of man he extends his quest, "beyond the God-belief". As it is hard to know why Faustus is unwilling to remain but man, so it is equally a philosophical checkmate why he chooses necromancy, he could well have chosen good to be otherwise. But perhaps he does so as a result of his imperfect understanding of the humanist's view of man that "man is his own rule and his own end". A tragic hero is wrong in the beginning, he commits error of judgement that conducts him to death, so the seeds of tragedy are sown in the beginning as the Chorus tells that Faustus chooses to go the Icarus-way and thus in the existing situation what remains to be seen is how he would be his own 'rule' and 'end' in the pursuit of his investigation, stretching beyond the limited knowledge and power of man.

The Prologue pronounces the theme—"Faustus's fortunes, good or bad" and then proceeds to introduce him as one born of "parents of base of stock" in a German town, called Rhodes, living a retired life. Marlowe then highlights his academic accomplishments how he studied divinity and soon earned in it a Doctorate degree at the University of Wittenberg. Thus, his profession is not soldiering or usury but divinity

So much he profits in divinity,
The fruitful plot of scholarism graced,
That shortly he was graced with Doctor's name,
Excelling all; and sweetly can dispute
In th' heavenly matters of theology.[4]

As per practice, a scholar's name was written in the *Cambridge Grace Book* when he was awarded a degree but in case of Faustus it does not mean the same as it meant to others. Faustus finds the existing learning inadequate to resolve certain problems pertaining to the realm of theology and astronomy and turns to magic books and thus the word 'grace' has a suggestion of irony. It is not the learning of divinity he acquired at the university but the dissatisfaction born of its limitations which brings its rejection. The move brings disgrace, disrepute, instead of renown and honour

For falling to a devilish exercise,
And glutted now with learning's golden gifts,
He surfeits upon cursed necromancy.[5]

Magic, says Harry Levin, "was originally the appurtenance of religion and when religion cast it off, it subsisted in the outer darkness along with appetite and curiosities which religion proscribed".[6] Faustus delights in the art of necromancy and sees in it the 'chiefest blisse'.

Nothing so sweet as magic is to him,
Which he prefers before his chiefest blisse".[7]

The stress on the word 'blisse' suggests that magic is to Faustus a source of power and pleasure as a crown was to Tamburlaine and gold to Barabas. The word 'reach' has a ring of satire. It is told that "heavens conspired his overthrow". But what heavens? Does it refer to the biblical divine seat of God or to what man creates by his own acts? Hell and heaven do not exist as territories but are states of mind and much depends on how man takes to them. The play's philosophy is neither wholly Christian nor paganistic but of synthesis between the medieval faith and the Renaissance knowledge which assures man the "inner tranquility that comes from an undivided mind". If Faustus ignores its truth, this is the tragic paradox of human intellect which is to be understood.

As the play advances, we discover Faustus in his study. He is one who is at the peak of his worldly power and is held in high esteem for his knowledge among his students. His common talk sound as aphorisms and bills are hung up as monuments, carrying within them something surpassing human wisdom. If it is so, why then does he become restless, why is he unwilling to remain "but Faustus and a man", and why does he feel an urge to command "All things that move between the quiet poles?" The medieval theology held that man is because he believes. To this the Renaissance answer was that man is because he thinks, acts and discovers. Neither view is wholly right or wrong to resolve Faustus's dilemma as Marlowe presents. In the world of tragedy, the hero can only take the road of experiment. He must follow his bent, take action and live it through. He feels the compulsion to realize himself fully in the face of all the odds and the test of his heroism is the degree of the risk he is willing to take. This connects the tragedy of Faustus with the tragedy of Adam. In the framework of Christian theology, the first man to be unparadised for seeking knowledge to be himself is Adam. It was a forward step in the direction of self-realization whereas in the eyes of orthodox people, it is sinful as Faustus's action is wholly devilish in the eyes of the Chorus. The significant words are "patient judgements" which we have to make upon his fortune, be it good or bad. The opening soliloquy is not a

Volponean invocation to his saint gold in its shrine of a usurer but "an inventory of the Renaissance mind"[8] in search of power. The soliloquy running for 62 lines ends with the attestation of belief and power in witchcraft.

A sound magician is a demi-god.[9]

But it underlines Faustus's sin which is the sin of mind "Swoln with cunning of a self-conceit". The two images of Phaethon (*Tamburlaine*) and Icarus (Faustus) are symbolic of human imagination, soaring too high to seek self-realisation but it is a pity that what the questers find is "more heat than light". Faustus's rejection of all studies but necromancy is highly dramatic but otherwise a very fascinating exercise to serve as a prelude to his sufferings which, as some hold, are not meaningless in that his coming into contact of evil will make him learn of what is good.

The meaning of the play is not only that Faustus's act is sinful and heretic, rather the meaning is the total field of the situation into which he walks of his own free will in accordance with the mysterious tragic urge of the time. Faustus is not a villain, in the accepted sense, 'conscienceless and heathen' but it is his arrogance and lust for power that drives him to the choice of necromancy. He reaches a level of perception which is hard to attain by the less venturesome individuals and as such his mind freely moves to traverse the forbidden realms. The words he cries out "How am I glutted with conceit of this", give a marvellous expression to the external elements of the Renaissance as he gloats over the power which he expects to acquire through magic. He says that he will make the spirits fly to India for gold and plunder the sea for orient pearls. This shows that in the subconscious he harbours a lust for gold also with little realization that this bourgeois evil of acquisitiveness will leave the seeker after truth in him a robber.

Shall I make spirits fetch me what I please,
Resolve me of all ambiguities,
Perform what desperate enterprise I will?

I'll have them fly to India for gold,
Ransack the ocean for orient pearl,

Faustus is very much optimistic about the success of the project that with the aid of magic he can get all ambiguities resolved and obstacles removed for the progression of human intellect and create what has been improbable for man to do in the course of history. For example, he talks of ridding the country of the foreign domination and fortify all Germany (Marlowe's Germany is England) with a wall of brass which is a noble idea of national interest. Equally the desire of clothing the school boys in silk, one can say, is a humanitarian gesture but it is in contravention of getting the other basic needs of human survival fulfilled.

I'll have them wall all Germany with brass,
And make swift Rhine circle fair Wittenberg.
I'll have them fill the public schools with silk,
Wherewith the students shall be bravely clad.
I'll levy soldiers with the coin they bring,
And chase the Prince of Parma from our land,
And reign sole king of all the provinces.[10]

The state of mind of Faustus before the execution of the bond is Marlowe's triumph of human psychology. He introduced the element of struggle in the tragedy for the first time to bring the performance closer to life. The power-play of the forces of good and evil within man is used as a device to probe deeper into the layers of the subconscious to reflect reality of man as he is in such crucial moments. Faustus hears something sounding in his ears: "Abjure this magic, turn to God again." Faustus is shaken, not because he fears the words of the Good Angel but because the act of choosing between faith and unfaith is by nature a hard challenge which only the venturesome persons dare to accept. He dismisses God as "vain fancies" and turns to a new God—"The God thou servest is thine own appetite." Such a concept of God lies outside the Christian theology and for want of moral sense tends to be an exercise in the romantic affirmation of self which humanism discourages. He says that he will raise an altar to worship the new God and offer the blood of the new-born babes. This shows that the new God is not all-loving and kind but a reflection of Milton's Moloch, a "horrid king besmeared with blood/ Of human sacrifices and parents tears." He questions his own self as to why he is wavering. He feels like turning to God again but the thought that a heretic is unloved by God desists him from taking such a decision.

Ay, and Faustus will turn to God again
To God? He loves thee not.
The God thou servest is thine own appetite,
Wherein is fixed the love of Belzebub
To whom I'll build an altar and a church
And offer lukewarm blood of new-born babes.[11]

Despite the warning of the Good Angel to "leave that execrable art" and think of heaven and heavenly things, Faustus thinks of "honour and of wealth" as advised by the Evil Angel. Evil has its own fascination, the temptation is too strong. The vacillation dies out and Faustus is resolute to sign the deed in blood. The situation is highly precarious. After he writes a few words, the blood congeals which is symbolic of the hardening of spirit signifying death. It is an omen of damnation which becomes discernible in death—soliloquy when the drop of Christ's blood that would save his soul is denied to him. Mephistophilis, fearing the loss of a soul, since the point is to enlarge the kingdom of Lucifer, brings a chafer of coals to melt the blood and Faustus puts his signature. Marlowe employs the theatrical device to heighten the tragic intensity of a bewildered self caught in hallucination: Faustus sees a mysterious inscription, "Homo fuge" on his arm whereas the fact is that there is nothing writ on it. The vision is fractured and the power of seeing has grown myopic under the impact of the resultant fears of selling the soul to the devil. The whole situation is symbolic to suggest what happens to man on his entry into the "forbidden" to overcome limitations without which he feels he cannot be what he aspires to want to be. In the beginning, the debate about the choice of study has hardly anything in it of 'worth' serious attention in Aristotelian sense but when the conflict of choice is resolved and Faustus becomes willing to barter his soul to gain unlimited power saying

> Had I as many souls as there be stars
> I'd give them all for Mephistophilis,
> By him I'll be great emperor of the world.[12]

the action becomes serious. We have a sense of shock and horror to see the blood refuse to flow. Thus, Faustus's bargain is a forward step of a 'sceptical reasoner' who is out to measure his strength against nature.

Thus, by the end of Act I, Faustus slips into a new role of a necromancer to read the secrets of nature. Marlowe knows that the power Faustus has acquired is a power minus God and carries with it the inevitable curse of damnation but he has left him with freedom to choose to see the truth of man by his own eyes rather than accepting like the medieval man what came to him from an outer agency. The bond has cut him from the normal scale of humanity. There is no significant action now to take place and the play, in the words of Cleanth Brooks, "will not be so much dramatic as elegiac".[13] Henceforth, Faustus is the man with no place to go and nothing to do really worthy of the supernatural powers that he feels he has come to possess. The last clause of the agreement—"And always be obedient to my will"—turns topsy turvy: the obedient servant becomes the master. It is Mephistophilis who speaks with the great authority of Lucifer and Faustus obeys. One wonders whether the knowledge he has gained in exchange of soul is knowledge or 'shadow' of knowledge. But soon he lapses into luxury and buffoonery because all that happens to him, after the pact is signed, is the devil's work. Only a fool can harbour the fond illusion that any power outside human agency can make miracles fall from the sky or that truth could be elicited from the father of lies.

As Marlowe was aware of the dilemma of the Renaissance man who little understood that the notion of self-sufficiency as revealed by humanism, if abused, will end in the reversal of high values set upon his powers, so Mephistophilis seems to have a penetrating insight into the mechanism of human mind: he knows how to keep a person in perpetual state of despair who is willing to fall and who is vacillating between the gratification of his appetites and fear of a God whom he has rejected without denying.

Faustus is curious to know about the place to which he has surrendered himself. He asks, "Tell me where is the place that men call hell" Mephistophilis's answer does not point to the traditional hell which God cut as Space no. 2 out of chaos for the rebellious angels to perpetually confine with which Faustus is well conversant and thus Mephistophilis's answer "under the heaven" strikes vague and cryptic. He says,

> Hell hath no limits, nor is circumscribed
> In one self place. But where we are in hell,
> And where hell is there must we ever be
> And to be short, when all the world dissolves
> And every creature shall be purified
> All places shall be hell that is not heaven.[14]

Mephistophilis's words "hath no limits/ but where we are is hell" are charged with the overtones of humanism and are of vital significance in that they are dropped from the mouth of the devil's disciple. They take the discussion out of the framework of Christian theology to set the wrong right in what the scriptures tell: Mephistophilis defines hell as a state of mind, not a territory as the new knowledge holds which is wholly man's creation and finds attestation later in Milton's Satan's description of hell also.

> The mind is its own place and in it self
> Can make a Heaven of Hell, a'Hell of Heaven.[15]

And, therefore, the question whether the voice is of Mephistophilis or of Marlowe is irrelevant to ask. At places in the play it is Marlowe's articulation which, for its departure from the biblical concept of hell and heaven was taken by the orthodox as unholy and impious and for it, if he was styled as an atheist, it is a different story. There are critics, Hazlitt is one, who have demolished the charge of atheism,[16] laid against him and find in his plays "no proofs of atheism or impiety attributed to him".[17]

Mephistophilis's explanation that when one is away from God, it is hell, is rooted in the theocentric concept of the universe. The person is doomed as he is and so is Faustus by that standard but because he has already rejected God, such a notion of hell strikes absurd. And what he adds is that if hell is limited to "sleeping, eating, walking and disputing" he is willing to be damned which is a surrender, not only of the soul but also of the body, to the devil. Cleanth Brooks calls it "self-aggrandisement" which is his basic motivation and which "ensures that the power he has gained will be used for what frivolous purposes". It is contrary to the spirit of the project he professes to undertake in the opening soliloquy, "Here, tire my brains to get a deity" and one wonders if he is aware of it. One can ask: if the new knowledge fails him, what could be the other means to attain "knowledge of a more ultimate kind" outside what he is locked into? The truth is that there seems to be nothing either way. The choice and the urge to transcend mortal limitations and be the very god is very much in accord with the intellectual and the spiritual spirit of the time, the project is an acid test of his heroism and therefore what sustains our interest is whether he gains divinity he aspires for or demeans his very humanness.

Marlowe brings in the issue of Lucifer's fall for Faustus' illumination but he, being a lost soul, learns nothing from this humanist discourse of moral significance of the devil who has seen the face of heaven and the darkness of hell. His version of the truth of heaven and hell is empirical the age was eager to accept. Faustus questions Mephistophilis "why Lucifer fell". The answer that it was the result of "aspiring pride and insolence" and that he himself is one of the "unhappy spirits" who fell with Lucifer is sufficient to warn Faustus of the danagerousness of the bargain. But it is a situation which he has chosen himself to walk into, aspiring to be more than human. The question is crucial in the sense that it seems to be directed more toward Faustus' fall rather than Lucifier's which is also hinted at in the Prologue in Icarus-imagery.

Mephistophilis is much moved while talking of the loss of the bliss of heaven, the tone grows of regret and he feels as if his soul is fainting.

> Think'st thou that I who saw the face of God,
> And tasted the eternal joys of Heaven,
> Am not tormented with ten thousand hells,
> In being deprived of everlasting bliss?
> Oh Faustus, leave these frivolous demands.
> Which strike a terror to my fainting soul.[18]

The whole thing is symbolic, as the orthodox would have it, of how the soul, when cut off from its divine source, is impoverished. The thrust of Mephistophilis's eloquence is a sort of advocacy in support of the moral choice of the Good Angel. Faustus is much surprised to see the devil so much on the side of the Angel. However, its psychological implication is not undermined. The venture to understand the metaphysics of good and evil is a test of his heroism on way to seeking self-realisation. In Renaissance which is the age of reason and Enlightenment the belief in the existence of the ghosts and the spirits was an anachronism, yet Marlowe creates a situation in which Faustus' pact with the devil does not look backward-looking, nor their interplay in human action appears as mere manifestations of Faustus' state of mind, they look as realities so long as we are in the theatre. Their visitation has psycho-spiritual associations: they are seen by one with whom they have some purpose and relation with his state of mind. In fact, the problem with Faustus is that his mind is drugged by the dreamy vision to be the superman which amounts to overstepping limitations and he is damned. And, therefore, he is not exonerated from the responsibility of his own damnation. Cleanth Brooks has also rightly observed that "it is not so much that God has damned him as that he has damned himself".[19]

Douglas Bush points out that the classical humanists took little interest in science for the reason that "they were concerned, not with man's control over nature but with the much harder problem of man's control over himself".[20] They found man behaving contrary to the ethical idealism of the ancient moralists which is seen in the writings of Machiavelli and other humanists who wrote "what men do and not what they ought to do". Harry Levin reads the play as "a tragedy of a scientific libertine who gained control over nature while losing control of himself"[21] and one wonders what nature Faustus 'gained control over' and what he lost. The truth is that it is the intellectual curiosity which seduced Faustus to be an ally of the devil. And thus his laments over the bargain to blame his alma mater "O would I had never seen Wertenberg: never read books" is a high piece of comedy. In the last soliloquy he also talks about burning 'books', one is in a dilemma what books he refers to—the books on necromancy or the whole learning he accumulated at the university.

It is Faustus' anthropocentrism that his imagination, after the bargain is made, runs in a rather random fashion from one object to another, having no element of consistency and logicality which is manifest in leaving out so serious a discussion and moving to make demand of a wife "the fairest maid in Germany", knowing that the demand is against the text of the pact[22] he has made to the devil. He says, "I am wanton and lascivious and cannot live without a wife". Mephistophilis himself is very much surprised to see his parasite talk of an object that belongs to a world of which he is no more a denizen, a world in which a wife assures a bond of humanity and exercises a humanizing impact on man. He persuades Faustus not to think of a woman and the bliss of marriage which is a sound piece of advice but fraught with irony in that the good is found where it is not to be found.

Tut, Faustus, marriage is but a ceremonial toy
If thou lovest me, think no more of it.
I'll cull thee out the fairest courtesans
And bring them every morning to thy bed.
She whom thine eye shall like, thy heart shall have
Be she as chaste as was Penelope

As wise as Saba, or as beautiful
As was bright Lucifer before his fall.[23]

Mephistophilis knows that marriage is not a ceremonial toy, nor something to be trifled with but he interprets the whole thing from the standpoint of a hedonist who is keen to glut his appetite. The dig is apparent and one asks: the indictment is of Mephistophilis or of Marlowe? Nevertheless seeing Faustus resolute, Mephistophilis brings a devil, dressed as a woman who looks like a 'hot whore', with fireworks attached to the body which, when explode, degenerates his trial of newly-obtained powers into a farce. The moral damage involved in Mephistophilis' promises to bring "the fairest courtesans" every morning to his bed is beyond the understanding of Faustus that marriage and "the fairest courtesans" are "incompatibles", they cannot go side by side. Marriage is a sacrament and involves responsibilities, love and reciprocity which Faustus in his demand is unwilling to share.

Thus, Faustus' request of procuring a bride is met with a refusal but the episode otherwise has moral implications, showing a voluptuary on the way to damnation. Humanism holds man imperfectable yet one who can effect his own salvation/ damnation right 'here and now'. If Faustus, as an aspiring rebel, chooses something otherwise to seek fulfillment it fits into Marlowe's view of man. But where his hero turns to false humanism, the dramatist parts company.

Faustus' disputations with Mephistophilis on divine astronomy, though verge on irony in that, it involves the dramatist's dilemma "that he cannot display more knowledge than man possessed", point to a heightened state of consciousness he has reached. The comicality of the situation is that Faustus underrates human intellect and rests on an agency to settle doubts whose identity is yet to define. Does Faustus not know the answers well of all those questions he might put to his mentor? And if he finds human intellect imperfect can any agency outside his own perfect it? Hence, what point is left there to show that he should feel so cheated? The queries are illuminating, no doubt, and have a ring of gravity because there are so many things, lying hitherto unexplored for man to unravel their mystery like the visitation of the ghost in *Hamlet*. Hamlet who by coincidence happens to be the student of Faustus's own University of Wittenberg, asks Horatio not to feel vexed over the visitation of the spirit since

> There are more things in heaven and earth, Horatio
> Than are dreamt of in your Philosophy.[24]

The question pertaining to the variations in the occurrences of the eclipses, oppositions, conjunctions, aspects differing from year to year is answered in Latin—*Per inacaqualem motum respectu tutius*—and Faustus feels satisfied. But the most crucial question—Who made the world?—is yet to be resolved for the reason that naming God as the creator is like accepting His sovereignty which is against the very law of Lucifer's kingdom, Mephistophilis is thus bound by the morality of hell, not to articulate the Christian view of the origin of the universe and thus the debate remains a travesty of the battle of wits, a cat and mouse play, ending in disillusionment, far greater than that of Barabas and Edward.

> FAUSTUS: Tell me who made the world?
> MEPHISTO: I will not
> FAUSTUS: Sweet Mephistophilis, tell me
> MEPHISTO: Move me not, for I will not tell thee.
> FAUSTUS: Villain, have not I bound thee to tell me anything?
> MEPHISTO: Ay, that is not against our kingdom, but this is.
> Think on hell, Faustus, for thou art damned.[25]

In fact, the play is Marlowe's answer to the debate that raged during the 16th century between the two opposing models of Christianity, fighting for supremacy: one was the orthodox Catholic view which upholds the value of faith, prayer, repentance and individual efforts in seeking salvation. The opposing current was that of the Calvinistic theology which held that each man is marked for salvation or damnation and nothing can alter the course of original destiny.

One may express fear whether repentance can cancel out the clauses of the bargain. Mephistophilis, one can say, is of the Devil's party but he is fully alive to the humanistic fervour that places a high price on human dignity. He holds the primacy of man over the supernaturalistic connotations of hell and heaven. He tries to impress upon Faustus that man is more excellent than heaven and therefore, instead of fixing his gaze toward heaven, it is wise for him to look into his own self to keep his humanity intact. It is an indirect hint to seduce him into repentance so that after he is freed from the bargain, he might live life fruitfully. The point is, therefore, not to be sceptic about the spiritual efficacy and the value of repentance, Mephistophilis' promptings are moral and have a ring of sincerity.

FAUSTUS: When I behold the heavens then I repent,
And curse thee, wicked Mephostophilis,
Because thou hast deprived me of those joys.
MEPHISTO: 'Twas thine own seeking, Faustus, thank thyself.
But think'st thou heaven is such a glorious thing?
I tell thee, Faustus, it is not half so fair
As thou or any man that breathes on earth.

Though Mephistophilis' explanation should have been sufficient to convince Faustus, yet he asks him to prove what he claims. The logic that Mephistophilis advances to substantiate his view of man in relation to the universe, as the humanists hold, is very simple, though traditional, having its own theological significance.

FAUSTUS: How prov'st thou that?
MEPHISTO: 'Twas made for man; then he's more excellent.
FAUSTUS: If heaven was made for man, 'twas made for me.
I will renounce this magic and repent.[26]

Therefore, if Faustus resolves to repent, it is not something surprising. It is an opportunity for him to right the wrong but as a result of his alliance with the devil his sensibility and good sense are destroyed. That is why he is easily trapped into the legalism of the Evil Angel that, since he is a 'spirit' as it was mentioned in the first clause of the bargain, he is not a subject of redemption and God will not pity him if he repents. And once again Faustus lapses into despair. But the imagination turns feverish. He hears the fearful echos—'Faustus' thou are damned[27]—whereas the fact is that there is no one to speak to him, it is hallucination. He sees in a vision "swords, knives, poison, guns, halters and envenomed steel", suggesting him the idea of suicide which he drops the moment he looks back to measure out the fruits of the accomplished deeds that he has performed as a necromancer. There is a sudden upsurge of hubris, he become aware of the "sweet pleasure" that the art of necromancy yields and has the capacity to redeem despair. He collects himself and the idea of seeking salvation by way of repentance is dismissed.

> Have not I made blind Homer sing to me
> Of Alexander's love and Oenon's death?
> And hath not he that built the walls of Thebes
> With ravishing sound of his melodious harp
> Made music with my Mephostophilis?
> Why should I die then, or basely despair?
> I am resolved, Faustus shall not repent.[28]

He sees no point in feeling despaired and asks Mephistophilis to continue the debate on astronomy. In fact, the problem with him is the lack of self confidence and the resultant instability of mind. Reason which is a never-failing friend of man is dulled and he fails to discriminate between the pleasures of illusion and reality. And thus if not he, at least, we see his dream of supreme felicity and drunkenness of power turning upside down, he is on verge of sinking into the abyss of darkness and perdition. In utter despair, he thinks of dissociating himself from Mephistophilis and asks him gingerly to go back to his rightful place which is "ugly hell" and holds him responsible for his damnation. What a lame excuse!

Marlowe as a humanist is well aware of human imperfectability and the ironies of 'free thinking' in case it happens to overstep limitations. Hence, it is no wonder if Faustus aims at becoming the very superman, without ever being conscious of the irony involved in such flights of romantic exuberance and a passion for unlimited freedom. Evil is inherent in man but it is not that it is irremedial. Faustus' rejection of God which incurs the charge of atheism is not so serious as what he does later after the bargain is made. That is why what happens to him during the process becomes a point of moral scrutiny for us to judge his failure or success. What an irony that in order to get even a minor query settled he has to depend on Mephistophilis' humour who keeps him beating down regularly with words of annoyance and dismay!

FAUSTUS: Ay, go, accursed spirit to ugly hell.
'Tis thou hast damned distressed Faustus' soul.
Is't not too late?
(Enter the Good and Evil Angles)
EVIL ANGEL: Too late
GOOD ANGEL: Never too late, if Faustus will repent.
EVIL ANGEL: If thou repent devils will tear thee in pieces.
GOOD ANGEL: Repent, and they shall never rase thy skin.
(Exeunt Angels)
FAUSTUS: Ah, Christ my saviour,
Seek to save distressed Faustus' soul.[29]

Faustus as a sinner invokes Christ but it is a human utterance which shows that he is still a man. As free thinker, he has not escaped the necessity of choice, the path he follows is of his own choosing which he is free to change any moment. It has not completely shut him out from all knowledge and experiences man could aspire for. Nevertheless, the hollowness of his bargain is emphasized in respect of any intellectual progress or enlightenment arrived at. But one may ask: who disappoints Faustus—Marlowe or Mephistophilis or neither? His failure too has its fruits of experience in the sense that it represents "in language and dramatic form the revelation of a knowledge beyond the reach of human wisdom".

What happens in the middle of the play, as the Chorus tells, is all about Faustus' launching into the world with Mephistophilis in a chariot drawn by the dragons to find the secrets of astronomy and "to prove Cosmography/ That measures coasts and kingdoms of the earth". The episode in which Faustus is seen in Rome, on the occasion of the holy Peter's feast is designed with a purpose which is not to raise laughter but to expose the greed and ignorance of the clerical class. They enter Pope's privy chamber and what they see there is very much shocking—a show of utter monstrosity and moral backwardness. Faustus becomes invisible and makes a show of his 'cunning' to Pope. The belief in the existence of ghosts and spirits in the Renaissance points to their intellectual sterility and frivolousness. And the power of show that Faustus displays, to the utter dismay and fear of the guests, is a travesty of the mission with which he embarked upon to be as great "on earth as Jove is in the sky/ Lord and commander of these elements".[30] The episode ends with Pope's retiring with his train, Faustus also returns home, the Chorus tells, after having taken the view "Of rarest things and royal courts of kings,/ He stayed his course and so returned home.[31]

The humanist emphasis on the secular virtues does not mean to undermine the religious values. Faustus' displacement from the centre to the periphery brings despair which Marlowe sketches in stages. Faustus calls himself a 'wretch' and questions the value of his action—'what hast thou done?' He sees no possibility of redemption and feels that the hour has come for him to cease to exist. He curses necromancy as 'Damned art'.

> Damned art thou, Faustus, damned: despair and die!
> Hell calls for right, and with a roaring voice
> Says "Faustus come! thine hour is almost come!"[32]

He sees suicide the sole alternative to be out of it. This shows that he has no place to go and even the supernatural powers that he has come to possess are of no use. As a matter of truth, Faustus was damned the moment when he signed the contract in blood and thereafter nothing remains for him to do worthwhile except experiencing failure and frustration. Sensing the right moment Mephistophilis gives him a dagger to ensure his damnation. Marlowe brings in a new character at this moment, he is an Old Man who represents the voice of the orthodox Christian church and faith in the value of repentance and prayer which have the power to save the soul even of an inveterate sinner. He sees an angel hovering over Faustus' head to pour grace into his soul and persuading him to avoid despair which leads to self slaughter, a sin of purgatory, as the Scriptures tell

> Oh stay, good Faustus, stay thy desperate steps.
> I see an angel hover o'er thy head,
> And with a vial full of precious grace,
> Offers to pour the same into, thy soul.
> Then call for mercy and avoid despair.[33]

In this hour of distress and spiritual tormentation, Faustus looks upon the Old Man as "my sweet friend", the words have a ring of sincerity and create a vision of heaven. Faustus asks him to leave him alone for sometime to ponder on his sins. He broods over his sinful past and thinks of doing something worthwhile to escape death but fails. Why? It is so because the sources he could fall back upon are exhausted in state of estrangement from the spiritual centre of the Being. Faustus oscillates throughout between repentance and despair, "I do repent, and yet I do despair", which is the fruits of the self-destructive tendency in humanism. He sees hell striving "with grace for conquest in my breast" and asks "What shall do to shun the snares of death?"[34] Is he really interested to do something to escape death? And if he is, who desists him from doing so? The return to grace lies always open to a sinner and so it does to him.

When Mephistophilis accuses him of disobedience of Lucifer and threatens to tear his flesh piecemeal

Thou traitor, Faustus, I arrest thy soul.
For disobedience to my sovereign lord.
Revolt, or I'll in piecemeal tear thy flesh.[35]

the readiness with which he turns to seek pardon for offending Lucifer is much dramatic. Lest the action should become melodramatic Marlowe relates it to the spirit of legality of the clause binding Faustus into slavery. The threat is sufficient to create shudder in the mind of a person who is already wavering between belief and unbelief. The moral exhortation of the Old Man is dropped arbitrarily as 'unjust'. He changes sides. Interestingly, Mephistophilis becomes 'Sweet Mephistophilis'. Faustus as supplicant urges upon him "to entreat thy lord/ To pardon my unjust presumption".[36]

The act of seeking pardon from God's adversary shows that now he is wholly of the devil's party and truly "a lost soul". He suddenly turns upon the Old Man, the 'sweet friend' of the earlier scenes becomes "base and crooked age". He beseeches Mephistophilis to torment him with pains which 'our hell' can afford.

Torment, sweet friend, that base and crooked age.
That durst dissuade me from thy Lucifer,
With greatest torment that our hell affords.[37]

The possessive pronoun 'our' shows Faustus as being himself a part of hell and his desire of subjecting the Old Man to physical tormentation is moral violence and therefore, hellish which marks a new development in the stages of his moral decay and regression.

What happens to one in state of divorce from the divine source is graphically picturised in a scene in which Lucifer enters in the room with Belzebub and Mephistophilis. Faustus is discovered with his servant, Wagner and the three scholars. The encounter between the human and the non-human is metaphysical in conception to reflect reality as to what being human implies. What the devils converse has a humanistic tinge and is not contrary to the scriptures—the soul thus sealed by sin in wantonness is a subject of hell.

LUCIFER: Those souls which sin seals the black sons of hell,
'Mong which as chief, Faustus, we come to thee,
Bringing with us lasting damnation
To wait upon thy soul. The time is come
Which makes it forfeit.

BELZEBUB: And here we'll stay,
To mark him how he doth demean himself.

MEPHISTO: How should he, but in desperate lunacy?
Fond worldling, now his heart blood dries with grief,
His conscience kills it, and his laboring brain
Begets a world of idle fantasies
To overreach the devil. But all in vain:
His store of pleasures must be sauced with pain.[38]

The thunder and the 'gloomy night' have sinister associations signifying death. Faustus is overwhelmed by a sense of isolation and a desperate malady which is spiritual. He sees in a vision the phantom of the devil and cries out. "Look sirs, comes he not? Comes he not?"[39] The scholars comfort him saying that "it is but a surfeit" and there is nothing to be feared. For the first time in the play he has a dialogue on normal human scale, his role of a demi-god is over. Till recently he has been behaving as if he were the lord of all creations but now the scholars seem to him more sweet and human than a prince or a king. They suggest him to look toward heaven and seek mercy but he knows that the doom is drawing near and thus his knees refuse to bend in prayer. The inertness is both physical and spiritual, Faustus' ruminations over what he has become after his self-anointed alienation from God are moral and point to the hazards of the anthropocentric humanism which are now beyond his powers to undo. He calls it a "A surfeit of deadly sin, that hath damned both body and soul."

The scholar advises him to seek God's mercy which is infinite, but he sees no escape from demnation for committing apostasy.

> But Faustus' offence can never be pardoned, The serpent that tempted Eve may be saved, But not Faustus.... Sweet friends, what shall become of Faustus, being in hell for ever?[40]

The scholar's suggestion urging upon Faustus to 'call on God', sounds hollow. Faustus is shaken and the reason is plain that he has rejected God, the will to undo the pact which is open to him is paralysed. The utterance is of utmost significance, fully in accord with the spirit of the theocentric humanism: the price one has to pay for blaspheming God.

> FAUSTUS: On God, whom Faustus hath abjured? On God, whom Faustus hath blasphemed? Oh my God, I would weep, but the devil draws in. my tears. Gush forth blood instead of tears, yea, life and soul. Oh, he stays my tongue. I would lift up my hands, but see; they hold them, they hold them.
>
> ALL: Who, Faustus?
>
> FAUSTUS: Why, Lucifer and Mephostophilis:
>
> Oh gentlemen, I gave them my soul for my cunning.[41]

Faustus hears the noise rise from nowhere and with it Mephistophilis becomes visible whom he calls 'bewitching fiend' and blames him for the seduction from the path of virtue. Mephistophilis makes a candid confession of having done so, his parting words have humanistic implications.

> What, weep'st thou? 'Tis too late, despair.
>
> Farewell.
>
> Fools that will laugh on earth, must weep in hell.[42]

As a matter of fact Faustus's problem was epistemological. The central questions in epistemology are: what can we know and how to know it? The questions are of intriguing nature since times were ripe for man to be sceptic about the old myths and beliefs. Faustus, as the Chorus tells, knows as much as is possible for man to know. The answer to the question—what can we know—is simple: what man is supposed to gain is the knowledge of life that makes him live life fruitfully within the bounds of the natural, i.e. earth-centred. There is nothing wrong if Faustus, like many, feels dissatisfied with the orthodox learning and intends to broaden the area of human understanding but there is every wrong with the means he chooses to do so. In fact, his choice of necromancy is an anachronism in the Renaissance when medieval world-order was collapsing and there was a great stirring in the sphere of human thought and action.

Knowledge is power 'knowing' and 'power' go hand in hand as Foucault elaborates. In other words, it is through the power that one can impress upon others his version of truth. But knowledge should be a man-centred programme and, when it is divorced from human context the entire venture tends to be ridiculous. Cleanth Brooks also points out that *Doctor Faustus* "is a play about knowledge about the relation of one's knowledge of the world to his knowledge of himself".[43] Faustus, being an intellectual, a sceptic, is a creation of the Renaissance striving for 'knowledge-infinite' and in the heat of enthusiasm makes a bargain with the devil to know what lies for man to know beyond human ken. The stage collapses and his every desire to know the unknowable is frustrated which shows that the "knowledge and felicity he has exchanged for shadows and for power he gets slavery".[44]

The death-soliloquy is almost commented upon by all the standard critics of Marlowe but the final philosophy that the play seeks to project they say, is not fully established. Rather it has made the conclusion more problematic. Which of the two warring views of Christianity is true to seek salvation—the Calvinistic doctrine of predestination or the belief in the spiritual efficacy of prayer, and repentance or both are found wanting when put to test in actual life situation? A.C. Ward has also observed, "No solution of the problem is proposed or even hinted at, any such was beyond both the poet and his times."[45] It is true that the problem which remains unresolved pertains to the domain of philosophy and is thus problematic by nature having no mathematical—like solution that two and two make four. But it is not all. The resolution which the play suggests lies in the 'middle state': to accommodate every new discovery with "the medieval notion of correspondence between the natural and the spiritual worlds."[46]

The play is to be interpreted not in the philosophy of religion or absence of religion but in the light of what actually happens to a man of flesh and blood that Faustus is and what he thinks of hell or heaven or what he does to exemplify the sufferings of a sinner on earth. Faustus begins in the spirit of modern scepticism, not to accept everything on dogma and dies as one showing faith in the opposite without fully comprehending the truth that the spiritual world is as real as the material world and dabbling in what is unearthly and subterranean is hellish.

With the fall of midnight Lucifer's men drag Faustus to hell and the orthodox would say that the end is a proper moral conclusion of the career of a voluptuary heretic. The myth of romancing with the devil, symbolic of vain fancies, gets exploded and the belief in the ultimate divine governance as held by the theocentric humanism is established. That is the devils or the mundane pleasures of the world cannot offer us greater satisfaction than God and religion and therefore denying their realities would mean endangering soul with no hope of salvation.

A high tragedy in Aristotelian sense brings illumination, not despair, the realization of the errors the hero commits in ignorance must take place at his own level. Faustus realizes the absurdity of the bargain and suffers but the suffering is not meaningless. He cries for soul's safety which shows that there remains in him a spark of the spiritual unsmothered. He says that he is willing to bear the incessant pains of hell for thousand years provided the soul is saved.

Let Faustus live in hell a thousand years,
A hundred thousand, and at last be saved.
Oh, no end is limited to damned souls.[47]

We wonder if he is the same Faustus who once was willing to offer Mephistophilis not one soul but "as many souls as there be stars" for gaining the supernatural powers.

In the beginning Faustus like an Epicurean was indifferent to 'an after-life'—"Thinkst thou that Faustus is so fond, to imagine/ That after this life there is any pain" but why he cries for the soul's safety now is a puzzle of theology. Is it illumination or the fear of the pains of hell? Or has he turned coward as a result of his long association with the devil that has wrought a great change in him? He knows that in a Christian cosmos the soul constitutes the identity and its divorce from the body, he prays for, is impossible. Even then his wish to be born as a brutish beast without a soul is a travesty of the bargain and therefore the plea of its dissolution, as Pythagoras philosophises, in the elements is absurd.

> Ah, Pythagoras' metempsychosis, were that true
> This soul should fly from me, and I be changed
> Unto some brutish beast.
> All beasts are happy, for when they die
> Their souls are soon dissolved in elements,
> But mine must live still to be plagued in hell.[48]

However, the whole exercise, if seen from the standpoint of the unbounded appetite for experience of the age, seems heroic but what benefits are accrued from the bargain is a subject of serious reflections.

The end heightens a situation, analogous to the Morality plays on the inverted scale and warns man to be moderate in ambition and love of pleasure. It is not the misuse of the Morality form in which there is a quest for heaven. Marlowe inverts the form to satirize man's quest for heaven which, in fact, turns out to be a quest for hell. Faustus is driven to despair and damnation against his will yet his cravings are not the cravings of an ignorant but of one who has learnt about the universal laws, governing human destiny in a theocentric universe.

NOTES

1. Nicholas Brooke, "The Moral Tragedy of *Doctor Faustus*" in *Casebook Series on Marlowe: Doctor Faustus*, John. Jump ((ed.), Macmillan, 1969, p. 119.
2. Philip Wayne, "Introduction" to *Faust, Part One*, Penguin Classics, 1949, p. 13.

   Part One of *Faust* was begun when Goethe was in his twenties and was finished when he was fifty one. Part Second, received its finishing touches when the poet was 83. This is the reason that in Part Second, idealism comes in to replace the romantic fervour.
3. A.C. Bradley, *Shakespearean Tragedy*, London: Macmillan, 1992, p. 20.
4. J.B. Steane (ed.), *Christopher Marlowe: The Complete Plays*, Penguin Books Ltd., 1969, p. 267.
5. *Ibid.*, p. 265.
6. Harry Levin, *Christopher Marlowe: The Overreacher*, London: Faber and Faber Ltd., 1954, p. 130.
7. *Doctor Faustus*, p. 268.
8. Harry Levin, *Christopher Marlowe: The Overreacher*, *op. cit.*, p. 134.
9. *Doctor Faustus*, *op. cit.*, p. 268.
10. *Ibid.*, pp. 268-69.
11. *Ibid.*, p. 279.
12. *Ibid.*, p. 276.
13. Cleanth Brooks, "The Unity of Marlowe's Doctor Faustus" in *Casebook Series*, *op. cit.*, p. 213.
14. *Doctor Faustus*, *op. cit.*, p. 283.
15. *Paradise Lost*, Bk-I, Lines 254-55.
16. The charge of atheism is one of the three heresies of Marlowe's unholy Trinity, the other two, being Epicureanism, fondness for good things of life and Machiavellianism, the will to power. Harry Levin says that "the Marlovian Trinity was based on positive, if heretical, premises, and its three articles of belief were closely related, if not interchangeable". Atheism, in the context of Marlowe, means rejection of God.

17. From "Lectures on the Age of Elizabeth" (1820) in *Complete Works*, ed. P.P. Howe. Quoted in *Casebook Series*, *op. cit.*, p. 28.
18. *Doctor Faustus*, *op. cit.*, p. 275.
19. Cleanth Brooks, "The Unity of Marlowe's Doctor Faustus" in *Casebook Series*, *op. cit*, p. 218.
20. Douglas Bush, *Preface to Renaissance Literature*, New York, W.W. Norton & Company, Inc., 1965, p. 20.
21. Harry Levin, *Christopher Marlowe: The Overreacher*, p. 158.
22. The source is the *English Faust Book*.

    "Hast thou not (quoth Mephistophilis) sworne thyself an enemy to God and all creatures? To this I answerer thee, thou canst not marry; thou canst not serue two masters, God, and my Prince: for wedlock is a chiefe institution ordained of God, and that hast thou promised to defie, as we doe all, and that hast thou also done: and moreouer thou hast confirmed it with thy blood: perswade thyselfe, that what thou doost in contempt of wedlock, it is all to thine owne delight." (Quoted in Helen Gardner, "The Theme of Damnation in *Doctor Faustus*" in *Casebook Series*, p. 98).
23. *Doctor Faustus*, *op. cit.*, p. 284.
24. *Hamlet*, Act II, sc.-I, lines 165-66.
25. *Doctor Faustus*, *op. cit.*, p. 287.
26. *Ibid.*, p. 285.
27. *Ibid.*, p. 287.
28. *Ibid.*, pp. 285-86.
29. *Ibid.*, pp. 287-88.
30. *Ibid.*, p. 268.
31. *Ibid.*, p. 303.
32. *Ibid.*, p. 329.
33. *Idem.*
34. *Idem.*
35. *Idem.*
36. *Idem.*
37. *Ibid.*, p. 330.
38. *Ibid.*, p. 332.

39. *Ibid.*, p. 333.
40. *Idem.*
41. *Idem.*
42. *Ibid.*, p. 334.
43. Cleanth Brooks, "The Unity of Marlowe's *Doctor Faustus*" in *Casebook Series*, *op. cit.*, p. 210.
44. Helen Gardner, "The Themes of Damnation in *Doctor Faustus*", *Casebook Series*, p. 99.
45. A.C. Ward, *A History of English Dramatic Literature* (1875), p. 336.
46. M.M. Mahood, *Poetry and Humanism*, p. 20.
47. *Doctor Faustus*, *op. cit.*, p. 337.
48. *Idem.*

5

The Jew of Malta

The second stage in the disintegration of the Renaissance humanism is man's wilful rejection of God, not God's rejection of man that drives Faustus, against his will to despair and hell and which Marlowe repeats in *The Jew of Malta*, shifting the scale of value from the sword power in Tamburlaine and the knowledge power in Faustus to the instinct of mercantilism in Barabas which fails him at the end for want of moral sense. The play dramatizes the fall of a man who is consumed by the lust for gold and warns, by implications, to be moderate in ambition so as to keep one's essential nobility intact. Marlowe's humanism brings into focus the dehumanizing impact of the inordinate passion for the riches on man and the resultant feuds and treacheries which destroyed the very foundations of life as much in the Jews as it did in the Christians, the Scythians and the Turks.

Why did Marlowe choose a wandering Jew the hero whose name has sinister associations?[1] Barabas for Marlowe is more than a representative of his race, a Machiavel who goes individualistic by dictating his own terms with the money power which has a socio-historical context in that when feudalism was on decline in Europe the rising class of the bourgeoisie were coming into prominence and becoming conscious of the significance of the capitalist mode of production as a means of expansion of individuality. Barabas is Marlowe's fine illustration of this great socio-economic upheaval which was both positivistic and negativistic—if it made man conscious of the mercantile power which once was looked upon as an obstacle to his entry into heaven, it also cut him off from the deepest foundation of life, the absence of which generated evil like individualism, lustfulness, economic warfare and the resultant cynical opportunism, egocentricity and craziness for power.

After the fall of Antwerp[2] (Belgium) in 1576, London which was the political as well as the literary capital of England became the habitation of all kinds of characters of diverse race, religion and nationality. There were businessmen, adventurers, swindlers, alchemists and speculators. Such a veritable hubbub of humanity provided the dramatist an opportunity to choose a character suiting his artistic philosophies. This is one vital factor that drama became highly realistic. For an artist who keeps an eye on the crude realism of the time with the contention that "the wheat and the tares grow together" the choice of a character of any sort is no accident. Barabas, the protagonist, appears as a Jew, suffering from the same moral malaise that destroyed the Scythian warrior and a very fine Christian scholar, he is as much a victim of the mysterious tragic urge of the time as any Renaissance man was.

The Prologue spoken at the court introduces the theme of the play; the story of a rich famous Jew who lived in Malta and who was "in all his projects a sound Machiavel, his ambition being more than modest". The cause of his destruction is clearly stated in the words "more than modest" which is over-ambitiousness and overlustfulness. As knowledge is power, so are the riches which, it is true, in themselves, are dumb and lame but makes the possessor walk and give articulation. This magic power of money becomes manifest in Mephistophilis's elaboration in Goethe's *Faust* (Part One) in a glaring metaphor.

> If I can pay for six stallions
> are not their powers also my own?
> I race about and a real man am I
> as if I had four and twenty legs.[3]

The young Marx analysed its implication in his *Economic and Philosophical Manuscripts* which is illuminating.[4] The impression that Mephistophilis creates is, in essence, the "magical enlargement of the radius of human action by means of money" such as Marx analysed.

Barabas is possessed by such a lust for wealth the shadow of which continues to darken the Jacobean stage also. The Jew becomes Volpone in Jonson's play, *Volpone or The Fox*, who is much alive to the benefits of this thriving commercial enterprise as Barabas. Volpone's invocation to saint gold in its shrine runs for 27 lines, he calls gold "the world's soul and mine". The power in the stallions is the power of money which man seeks to exploit for 'self-reliance' and 'self-expression' that characterized the age. The voice of Volpone in the concluding part of the Invocation seems to be Mephistophilis's promptings.

Dear saint,
Riches, the dumb god that giv'st all men tongues;
Thou canst do nought, and yet mak'st men do all things;
The price of souls; even hell, with thee to boot,
Is made worth heaven. Thou art virtue, fame,
Honour, and all things else. Who can get thee,
He shall be noble valiant, honest, wise—[5]

The Jew is a Maltese denizen (Malta being a strategic point on the old trade routes in the Mediterranean region) but his 'more modest' ambition at once makes him a fit character of Renaissance England. The play begins with the spirit of Machiavel, making his intention known to the audience that he has come in Britain, not to deliver a lecture but

to present the tragedy of a Jew
Who smiles to see how his bags are crammed.[6]

After the exeunt the ghost of Machiavel, the curtains rise and Barabas is discovered in his counting house. We are very much impressed by the manner in which he so contemptuously pushes away the 'paltry silverings' which is his booty collected from the helpless clients. He calls it 'the trash'.

Fie, what a trouble it is to count the trash.

but we know the reality. The truth is that it is the constant touch with the dumb riches that has turned him into a class simulator and hypocrite. He has grown insensitive to human emotions and feelings. Pope uses irony to define man, so does Marlowe before Pope did it. The first soliloquy is a brilliant piece of irony. Barabas's pose of disinterestedness in riches slips down when in the next minute he becomes aware of the worth of the precious stones.

> Bags of fiery opals, sapphires, amethysts,
> Jacinths, hard topaz, grass-green emeralds,
> Beauteous rubies, sparkling diamonds.[7]

Tamburlaine seeks delight by counting the conquered monarchies, Barabas gloats over the names of each costly stone he has collected by way of usury. But contrary to Tamburlaine's macrocosmic worldwide empery, his microcosmic world is the

> Infinite riches in a little room.

he draws power from. Nevertheless, he is cast in the same Tamburlainean mould with the difference that his sovereignty lies not in the crown but in the 'infinite riches'. He counts the names of the rich Jews in Greece, Portugal, France and Malta, including his own name and makes confession of their plight as to how they are kept away from the power because in the eyes of the Christians, they are 'a scattered nation'.

> I must confess we come not to be kings:
> That's not our fault: alas, our number's few,
> And crowns come either by succession,
> Or urg'd by force; and nothing violent,
> Oft have I heard tell, can be permanent.[8]

The confession points to the mysterious urge of the time he harbours in the subconscious to be an extraordinary individual in Malta by power of money. He does not consider it immoral if power comes by way of inheritance or by force.

The dimensions of Barabas's empire of fabulous treasures can be well measured by the quality of argosies which his ships are carrying, laden with the Persian silk, gold and orient pearls which are to reach Malta through the Mediterranean sea. Marlowe skilfully brings under focus the metamorphosis of one who is virtually a Tamburlaine of riches. A messenger comes to inform him about the safe riding of the ships with the request that he has to reach the Custom-House to clear the duties. Barabas is sure of the power of his 'golden magic wand', his word is a law in his own sphere. He asks the messenger to go back and tell the custom authorities that 'the Jew of Malta' has sent him for the clearance of the bills of entry and the ships discharged of the fraught.

> Go tell'em the Jew of Malta sent thee, man:
>
> Tush, who amongst 'em knows not Barabas?[9]

What a show of egotism and glorification of self! The Jew's aspiring soul wishes its identity to be known to the world, by 'the Jew of Malta' signifying the power, associated with money, rather than by a name 'Barabas', a human.

However, an upheaval comes in Malta with the arrival of the Turkish fleet and with it the real action of the play begins to unfold. As per practice of the political hegemony, the Maltese are to pay the arrears of the ten years' tribute to the Turkish prince, Selim Calymath. The Turkish bassoes come to the Senate House to urge the Governor, Ferneze, to make provision for the payment of the unpaid arrears. The Knights of Malta are given a month to raise the money. The Governor passes on the responsibility of the collection of the amount to the Jews with full justification.

As per articles of the decree each Jew has to pay one half of his estate or become a Christian and in case of denial he loses all that he has. Barabas denies to be a convertite but agrees to part with one half of his wealth. He smells some foul policy in the Governor's threat of 'seizure on all' and instantly resolves to counter it by 'policy', he calls it 'Realpolitik' which is the very spirit of Machiavel that is heard in the Prologue. The Jews are accused of corrupt practices to 'collect' almost unbelievable wealth by way of usury and Barabas is no exception. He wants his own riches to be spared and does not mind the affliction befalling his own men. A fine display of fellow-feeling and loyalty to the Jewish community! His protest, that other Jews could be tried for wickedness and dishonesty but not he, is highly individualistic which ironically alienates him from the Jewish community of Malta. The Governor (almost in Marlowe's voice) throws at him, much to his annoyance and dismay, moral exhortation to do away with covetousness which is a sin. But the Jew's retort turns on vengeance, guile and treachery that since he is being robbed by the Christians, he has the right to openly steal more and more. What a lame excuse of being dishonest and acquisitive!

FERNEZE: Excess of wealth is cause of covetousness;
And covetousness, O, 'tis a monstrous sin!
BARABAS: Ay, but theft is worse. Tush! Take not from
Me, then,
For that is theft; and, if you rob me thus,
I must be forc'd to steal, and compass more.[10]

However, before the Governor turns Barabas's house into a convent, the Jew has played his 'politik': he hides his pearls, jewels and stones under a plank in the upper chamber of the house and the buried treasure is marked ironically with a cross. Barabas, as a Jew, is held in high esteem among the Jews by virtue of his being fabulously rich. He has no family but a 14 year old daughter, Abigail whom, he says, he holds "as dear/ As Agamemnon did his Iphigen". And the depth of his love can well be measured by the role he assigns to her in his fight with the Christians to repossess the gold. As per plan, Abigail is to enter the nunnery as a nun under the pretence of being a sinner whereas the truth is that she is not a sinner at all. She is to throw the bags of infinite riches in the darkness of the night and he has to collect them like prized catch. The proposal is hellish and startling for Abigail to comprehend how one can play a dissembler and, as he desires, practice religion, not for holiness or spiritual purification but to camouflage 'mischiefs' from 'suspicion'.

ABIGAIL: How! as a nun?
BARABAS: Ay, daughter; for religion
Hides many mischiefs from suspicion

ABIGAIL: Ay, but, father, they will suspect me there.
BARABAS: Let 'em suspect, but be thou so precise
As they may think it done of holiness.
Entreat 'em fair, and give them friendly speech,
And seem to them as if thy sins were great,
Till thou hast gotten to be entertain'd.
ABIGAIL: Thus, father, shall I much dissemble.
BARABAS: Tush![11]

Abigail's placement is a part of Machiavel's policy to win back his lost treasure but it is a reflection of Barabas' attitude to religion which is limited to the preservation of the material, not the spiritual wealth. It is decided that Barabas is to reach the door of the house at dawn to collect his wealth which Abigail is to throw down. But it is Marlowe's insight into human psychology rather than morality that makes the whole episode dramatically suspense-ridden. The scene shifts to a street outside the nunnery. Barabas appears with a candle pouring forth 'fatal curses' upon the Christians.

Thus like the sad presaging raven that tolls
The sick man's passport in her hollow beak,
And in the shadow of the silent night
Doth shake contagion from her sable wings,
Vex'd and tormented runs poor Barabas
With fatal curses towards these Christians.[12]

The imagery well brings out the plight of an individual being tormented by the hysteria of wealth. Barabas is the 'sad presaging raven' shaking contagion from its 'sable wings', signifying sickness and death which is, in metaphorical sense, spiritual death. The Jew invokes God to help Abigail as He did the 'sons of Israel'. The essential incompatibility of the two situations renders the Jew's implorings absurd.

O Thou, that with a fiery pillar ledd'st
The sons of Israel through the dismal shades,
Light Abraham's offspring, and direct the hand

Of Abigail this night! Or let the day.

Turn to eternal darkness after this![13]

It is a case of distortion of the Scriptures which amounts to the charge of blasphemy but the Jew hardly feels the pangs of conscience since he is a Mammon-worshipper, not a devotee of Bibilical God. Since Barabas happens to reach before midnight when Abigail rises to search for the hidden treasure, he looks a grotesque figure, while directing Abigail.

BARA: But stay: what star shines yonder in the east?
The loadstar of my life, if Abigail.
Who's there?

ABIGAIL: Who's that?

BARA: Peace, Abigail! 'tis I.

ABIGAIL: Then, father, here receive thy happiness.[14]

Marlowe dramatizes the process of straightening the wrinkled psyche of a commercial baron at the recovery of his riches. The strategy as devised by the Jew to regain his treasure works. Bags fall from above into his hands and the very touch of it makes him break into hysterical ecstasy.

O Abigail, Abigail, that I had thee here too!
Then my desires were fully satisfied:
But I will practice thy enlargement thence:
O girl! O gold! O beauty! O my bliss![15]

The episode is significant in that what in Marlowe's time was heroic about business enterprise was not simple amassing of wealth but control. And thus in this context the Jew adumbrates both capitalist and capitalism.

The Jewish tradition as represented by prophets, like Amos and Hosea, discourages the pursuit of the doctrine of individualism and lays emphasis on the cardinal moral virtues like love, compassion, justice and sense of fellow-feelings. A Jew is defined as a figure in the Prayer book, used in most of the synagogues today that where there are tears and sufferings, the Jew weeps in all places. But Barabas's Jewishness is a facade. Whatever he utters in 'asides' shows him a different man. When he asks the Jews, "Why weep you not to think upon my wrongs", it is the display of 'policy' of self-centredness, cunning and falsity and partly of the satanic greed of gold which was widespread and which was dividing the society into classes. Why Barabas is interested to declass himself from the Jewish community? Because he is more aware of the capitalist significance of money as an extension of self than the other members of the class. We know that the other Jews are equally wronged but he is impervious to their loss because the very spirit of Hasidism[16] ceases to have for him any meaning at all. Barabas seems to be a votary of Nietzschean doctrine of individualism, he does not want his individuality to be obscured in the Jewish community.

You were a multitude, and I but one.

With the recovery of his wealth he is a boiling cauldron of hatred against the world he is planted in and the play takes on the trappings of a revenge tragedy. He abuses wealth as a power to wreck ruination on the enemy but it is a pity that during the process the devil takes possession of his heart and much of the goodness he happens to possess gets perverted. The impression is of waste and failure.

The convention of soliloquy and 'aside' as a stage device was very common in the Elizabethan drama, the purpose being the general exposition of the theme and partly to convey to the audience directly a character's inner motives and state of mind. In the 'aside', "Now will I show myself to have more of the serpent that the dove", Barabas's real self becomes unconsciously manifest that, despite all his gold, he remains what man was in "pre-capitalist romantic idyll", a savage. The animal imagery is Marlowe's degradation of man's greed for gold in general and of the Jew in particular who boasts of his being, not a fool but a rogue having no moral principles in life. The venom that the serpent in him spits out becomes more venomous when money power is added to it and put to disuse. It is said of Hamlet that the true Hamlet is in the soliloquies, so the Jew's reality is out in 'asides'. For example, when he claims that he is "framed of finer mould that common men". It is no secret that the mould he is cast into is of utter monstrosity and moral perversion which becomes all the more glaring in his visit to the slave-market where slaves are brought for sale. It is a show of the white coloniser's imperialistic myth of superiority over the dispossessed natives and this extravagant sight must have been enthusiastical and exhilarating for the Elizabethans. The scene is a fine product of Marlowe's imaginative entry into the obscure realm of psychology of a highly individualistic character. Each one's price is written on the back like commodities for ready purchase. Barabas's appearance is of much respite for the custodians since they hope that the Jew would "give us present money for them all". But it is otherwise a reflection of the bourgeois subjectivism of the expansion of self that the Jew imagines to be in 'owning property' by the right of purchase. Marlowe is well aware of the objective laws of the capitalist evolution and man's role in its development but his plea is to keep humanity intact which is all an individual matter.

Seeing the price of two hundred crowns tugged at the back of a Turkish slave, his quizzical query to the master, "What, can he steal, that you demand so much?" is not a simple reflection of the racial hatred and commercial greed. Is he really interested in one who can steal because he thinks that perhaps his own stealing is inadequate to satisfy the passion of revenge? He is interested in one who has the philosopher's stone to pluck for him miracles from the sky and who "is sickly an't be but for sparing victuals". At last he takes possession of one, he is Ithamore, born in Thrase and brought up in Arabia, for a hundred crowns. The manner in which he conducts the slave to follow him "Come, Sirrah, you're mine" is characteristic of the white European colonizer's jargon to treat the native as if, when dispossessed of his human identity, he were reduced to a commodity item.

It is with Ithamore as Barabas's accomplice that Marlowe digs at the Jew's antecedents, partly by bringing into focus his philosophy of education that he so fondly imparts to his disciple to pervert the good in him.

> First, be thou void of these affections:
> Compassion, love, vain hope, and heartless fear;

Be mov'd at nothing, see thou pity none,
But to thyself smile when the Christians moan.[17]

Here the Jew's anti-Christian bias becomes manifest. But whereas Ithamore's retort, "O brave master! I worship your nose for this", on the one hand, alludes to the Jew's grotesque facial make-up which is a reflection of the inner spiritual deformity, there the cunningly devised words that his profession is "what you please", on the other, show that he is not one entirely to have the soul of a slave but of a Machiavellian too. This partly determines Ithamore's identity that he could be the Jew's alter-ego, the extension of his self. In response to Ithamore's words of loyalty, Barabas gives an account of the villainies which sounds awful and shakes one's imagination to the roots. T.S. Eliot's observation that such a creation is a case of "prodigious caricature" is partly true—the following words bear testimony to it.

I walk abroad o' nights,
And kill sick people groaning under walls;
Sometimes I go about and poison wells;

The changing graph of the various professions is startling. As a man of medicine, Barabas recollects how he began

To practice first upon the Italian;
There I enrich'd the priests with burials
And always kept the saxton's arms in the ure.[18]

As an engineer, he "slew friend and enemy with my stratagems", and as an usurer he restored to

...extorting, cozening, forfeiting,
And tricks belonging unto brokery,
I fill'd the goals with bankrupts in a year,
And with young orphans planted hospitals;
And every moon made some or other mad,
And now and then one hang himself for grief,
Pinning upon his breast a long great scroll
How I with interest tormented him.[19]

Barabas thus seems a complex of various sorts of evils. But as evil begets evil, the account digs out the evil interestingly in Ithamore as well. He feels tempted to impress on his master's mind the nature of his destructive power which is sufficient to throw a man of Barabas's psychology into hysteria. He says he can easily set Christian villages on fire, chain eunuchs and bind the galley slaves. He romantically digs at his past, that when he was an hostler in an inn, in the night he secretly stole into the travellers' chambers to cut their throats. And once at Jerusalem, where the pilgrims 'kneel'd', he says, he

> strewed powder on the marble stones,
> And there withal their knees would rankle so,
> That I have laugh'd a-good to see the cripples
> Go limping home to Christendom on stilts.[20]

As such, the togetherness of the two such diabolic figures, be it an act of destiny or chance, is sinister as if evil is let loose on the Maltese population. For Barabas, the evil in Ithamore is 'something' he can fully exploit to turn the moral universe on his head. In order to derive the maximum out of this alliance he asks him to "account of me as of thy fellow" to win his confidence.

> We are villains both,
> Both circumcised. We hate Christians both.
> Be true and secret; thou shalt want no gold.[21]

After Ithamore's entry into the Jew's house, his passion for wealth is replaced by the passion of revenge. Even when some client is reported to have turned falsifier, he dismisses it so casually as if nothing happened.

Structurally, the plot, as per Aristotle's requirement should have a proper beginning, a middle and an end. *The Jew of Malta* is a play with a perfect middle, built on a series of misdeeds and crimes the Jew commits the genesis of which is the serpent-sting of wealth as he himself says and which leads to a natural end, i.e. the fall into a boiling cauldron. The first victims of their stratagem are the two young men, Don Lodowick, the Governor' son and Mafhias, a Maltese gentleman. The two are projected as Abigail's lovers. Barabas writes a forged letter in Lodowick's name to be delivered to Mathias expressing love for Abigail. The two are thus set as rivals against each other in a duel with the utterance that it "is no sin to deceive a Christian" as for him they are heretics and "Faith is not to be held with heretics". They fight and Barabas's promptings "O, bravely fought." are the devil's promptings, emanating disaster and gloominess. Cries are heard within "Part them, part them" and with Barabas's departure with the words, "Ay, part them, now they are dead", the episode ends which for Ithamore is the fruits of the "bravest policy of the master". Its full villainy is brought out by Ithamore to Abigail who is still unaware of the plot. He appears laughingly, much to Abigail's discomfiture and puzzlement.

ABI: Why, how now, Ithamore! Why laugh'st thou so?

ITHA: O mistress! Ha, ha, ha!

ABI: Why, what ail'st thou?

ITHA: O, my master!

ABI: Ha!

ITHA: O mistress, I have the bravest, gravest, secret, subtle, bottle-nosed knave to my master, that ever gentleman had!

ABI: Say, knave, why rail'st upon my father thus?

ITHA: O, my master has the bravest policy!

ABI: Wherein?

ITHA: Why, the devil invented a challenge, my master writ it, and I carried it, first to Lodowick, and imprimis to Mathia(s);
And then they met, (and,) as the story says,
In doleful wise they ended both their days.[22]

The ghastly revelation shakes Abigail to the roots for the reason that they were destroyed for 'my favour'. The father image collapses in her eyes and the Jew's identity is reduced to an "unkind Barabas!"

Hard-hearted father, unkind Barabas!
Was this the pursuit of the policy,
To make me show them favour severally,
That by my favour they should both be slain?[23]

Abigail feels disillusioned, orphaned and helpless. Her agonized cries expose the vileness of the Jew's pursuit of 'policy' which is void of any moral qualms and the transcendence of which is hard to accomplish.

But I perceive there is no love on earth,
Pity in Jews, nor piety in Turks.[24]

It is the degradation of man in a bourgeius society that values limitless individualism.

Marlowe's degradation of the Jew that takes place by stages is not limited to an individual or the race but to man who, in weaker moments, becomes oblivious of his sub-angelic heritage[25] and feels content to live life even if it comes to be of no moral significance. After Mathias and Lodowick, it is Abigail and the nuns who are destroyed by the passion of revenge. Abigail runs away from home to escape the devilish plotting of her father and enters the convent. When the letter bearing the news of her conversion reaches the Jew he throws aside all bonds of humanity and turns into a devil's disciple. The dramatist has closely followed the curves of the inner mechanism of his mind. What ails him is not Abigail's conversion but her advice of 'repentance' to him which shows that she has known the secret of the death of her two lovers. Abigail who was, a minute ago innocent and loving, becomes dramatically "False, credulous, inconstant Abigail".

What, Abigail become a nun again!
False and unkind! What, hast thou lost thy father?
And, all unknown and unconstrain'd of me,
Art thou again got the nunnery?
Now here she writes, and wills me to repent:
Repentance! Spurca! What pretendeth this?

I fear she knows—'tis so—of my device
In Don Mathias' and Lodovico's death.[26]

And since he has turned impervious to any sane suggestion, he immediately interprets it as a case of disbelief and betrayal of the umbilical ties, knowing that the relationship is reciprocal. The devil in him is up to destroy the very evidence (which is Abigail)

If so, 'tis time that it be seen into;
For she that varies from me in belief,
Gives great presumption that she loves me not,
Or, loving doth dislike of something done.[27]

The thought-process becomes all the more diabolic and perverted when he traps Ithamore into this ruinous plotting.

O Ithamore, come near.
Come near, my love; come near, thy master's life,
My trusty servant, nay, my second self;
For I have now no hope but even in thee,
And on that hope my happiness is built.[28]

The words are so carefully chosen that they can win anybody's confidence. We know that Ithamore cannot outwit his master's Machiavellanism. The affinity which the Jew intends to establish between the two selves is of gross opportunism, and self-aggrandisement. The Jew has already suffered humiliations and Abigail's adoption of Christianity is an additional injury he can hardly sleep over. She is thrown out of inheritance and blessings.

Ne'er shall she live to inherit aught of mine,
Be bless'd of me, nor come within my gates,
But perish underneath my bitter curse,
Like Cain by Adam for his brother's death.[29]

He knows that the predicament of the two—Cain and Abigail—is not similar: Cain murdered Abel, Abigail does not commit any such crime and Adam did not destroy Cain for Abel's murder as he thinks of murdering Abigail for no crime of her own. Thus, he brings in the Biblical parallel which is perhaps an attempt to justify the morality of the act. William Blake says that "Milton was of the devil's party without knowing it." Harry Levin also observes "Marlowe was never more the devil's advocate than when he chose a wandering Jew his hero". But the two situations are differing. Satan's adversary is God, the Almighty, and his stoicism is reflected in feeling content to be the Prince of Hell. The Jew's enemy is man himself, the evil in him, the transcendence of which is not to be effected by dogma but by acts (character) as the Unitarians would have it. Marlowe as a humanist is well aware of the orbit within which the self could move in state of moral quandary when cut off from its spiritual foundations.

Barabas' earlier acts of barbarism are dimmed by the heinous crime of mass-slaughter but they show his departure from the ethico-moral concerns in humanism. In order to destroy Abigail with her new faith, he devises a plot and throws over it the religious colouring to escape suspect of any foul play. As per practice in Malta, alms are sent to the nunnery on 'Saint Jaques' Even'. Barabas too wants to send his alms which is the poisonous porridge he has prepared by adding a precious powder he bought in Ancona. He asks Ithamore to carry it to the nunnery and set it in the midst of alms in such a manner that no enquiries are made as to "who hath sent it". The proposed reward is much alluring but deceptive, "My purse, my coffer and myself is thine" which is a subtle demonstration of the Jew's treachery and simulation. Ithamore makes no mistake in carrying out his master's direction. Consequently, all the nuns including Abigail are put to death. What is the Jew's state of mind after this gruesome tragedy is a point of interest. To Ithamore's query whether he feels sorrow for Abigails's death, the Jew's reply, "No, but I grieve because she lived so long", shows his utter callousness and surrender to the devil. The tone becomes disease-ridden and infranatural. How is it that he feels much relieved after this tragedy which the dramatist records by showing his attitude to the chiming of the church-bells which earlier sounded harsh and jarring like "tinkers' pan" but now they sound sweet and comforting?

However, the situation still persists to be precarious for the Jew. It is learnt that Abigail, before she died, gave the forged letter to Friar Barnardine and told all about the secret of killing of Mathias and Lodowick by arranging a duel. The Friars and the monks are not favourably drawn, they are projected more as the creatures of this mundane world rather than of the spiritual to act as torch-bearer for the laity. Barnardine's grief, it is learnt, is not that Abigail died but that she died a virgin's death. Ithamore intends to poison the monks, perhaps for their dubious morality and the Jew's assurance that he need not do so because "now the nuns are dead/ They'll die with grief"[30] becomes all the more a grim comment on the moral position of the clergy.

Barabas now turns to Barnardine's destruction because he is one who harbours the secret of his crime. He takes Ithamore aside and tells him about Abigail's confession of their diabolism and if something is not done they are both ruined. But since the Machiavel in him, in opposition to the spirit of humanism, keeps changing its mode of operation from situation to situation the Jew's resolve to play a dissembler shows that the spirit of satanic energy and vindictiveness is not dissipative in him. The dissembler in him takes guard to combat the precariousness of the situation. His readiness to embrace Christianity is a subtle dramatic pose which exposes his own religious position. The truth is that he is true neither to Judaism, nor to Christianity but to Lucifer which is a parody of the Christian idea of redemption. The gods he worships are not the deities of the classical antiquity but gods of gold and to them his services are bound. In the beginning, he refused to be a convertite but now he is willing to join a monastic order and is ready "to whip myself to death" and do penance for "my sin". But does he really consider that what he has done is sinful? Nevertheless, this is sufficient to speak of his hypocrisy and fraud and if the friars fail to see through its mechanism, the fault lies with them, not with the Jew, being true to nature as it is. He cries out as if he is a hardened sinner and in need of a holy man's spiritual succour for redemption of his soul.

O holy friars, the burden of my sins
Lie heavy on my soul! Then, pray you, tell me,
Is't not too late now to turn Christian?
I have been zealous in the Jewish faith,
Hard-hearted to the poor, a covetous wretch,
That would for lucre's sake have sold my soul.
A hundred for a hundred I have ta'en;
And now for store of wealth may I compare
With all the Jews in Malta: but what is wealth?
I am a Jew, and therefore am I lost.
Would penance serve for this my sin,
I could afford to whip myself to death.[31]

Since the Jew is a Renaissance man of action, not a medieval figure bowing calmly to the onslaught of fatality, the manner in which he fights evil with greater evil is barbaric and has no moral sanction of the civilized world. The cries of a sinner in him verge on comicality. He looks a comic character. He says that he is willing to die as a martyr for the sin of covetousness by doing penance but the reality is otherwise. Wilbur Sanders has rightly pointed out that the "the comic texture is very dense but one perception that hovers at the edge of laughter is that Barabas' use of the language of religion and piety as a weapon against the personal and commercial enemies is not different in kind from the use of that language elsewhere".[32] Ithamore seems to be an extension of the Jew's subconscious and thus his fears that perhaps "penance will not serve" are Jew's fears.

The Jew has had a taste of gold and is well aware of its magic power which is hard for man to resist. He plans the seduction of the two Friars—Barnardine and Jacomo—by throwing the bait of gold that he offers his wealth in charity to a 'religious house' and would live an ascetic's life of fasting and prayer for the purification of the spirit.

To fast, to pray, and wear a shirt of hair,
And on my knees creep to Jerusalem.
Cellars of wine, and sollars full of wheat,
Warehouses stuff'd with spices and with drugs,
Whole chests of gold in bullion and in coin,
Besides I know not how much weight in peral,
Orient and round, have I within my house;
....
Great sums of money lying in the banco.
All this I'll give to some religious house,
So I may be baptiz'd and live therein.[33]

The stage for the destruction of the two Friars is set. Barnardine and Jacomo vie with each other in describing the merits of their respective order. It is again the lust for gold that reduces the 'supposed' holiness to a rat-race pursuit of gold. He knows that the choice of one's order for baptization will rouse the jealousy of the other. As such, he asks Jacomo to come to his house "at one o'clock this night" which opens for the Friar a vision of fabulous wealth. Neither wants to leave the place and when Barnardine calls Jacomo a 'rogue', a fight ensues which is much amusing and ironic. Ithamore urges the Jew to part them and the Jew's comment "This is mere frailty"[34] is Marlowe's dig at the fallen image of the clergy. However, Jacomo leaves the place and Barnardine stays back with great expectations to gain possession of wealth without ever being suspicious of the Jew's satanism. Barabas' strategy is plain that Barnardine must die who, he thanks, is responsible for the conversion of Abigail before Jacomo comes. Barnardine is strangulated and at Ithamore's suggestion the dead Friar is set upright against the wall leaning upon the staff in hand "as if he were begging of bacon". It is one o'clock and Jacomo, as if lust incarnate, enters with soaring aspirations and eager to convert the Jew and secure his gold for his order.

O happy hour, wherein I shall convert
An infidel, and bring his gold into our treasury![35]

Seeing the leaning Barnardine on the staff, Jacomo at once concludes that perhaps he stands there in this posture to block his way and inflict some wrong on him. Jacomo's consciousness is drugged by the vision of acquisition of Jew's wealth. He strikes him hard with his staff and when the Friar's dead body falls forward, Ithamore and his master appear dramatically on the scene to stand as witness to the crime. What then goes off between the two looks as if the whole thing is a prearranged comedy. Ithamore's query to the master whether he would like to embrace Christianity even after having seen so vulgar a drama of human lust and bestiality, the Jew's laconic utterance that he would rather remain a Jew is a calculated move, not to part with a brick of his empire.

ITH: Fie upon 'em! Master, will you turn
Christian, when holy friars turn devils and murder one another?

BARA: No, for this example I'll remain a Jew.
Heaven bless me! What, a friar a murderer!
When shall you see a Jew commit the like?[36]

The Jew refuses to let Jacomo slip out saying "No pardon me, the law must have his course" and the poor Friar is executed as a criminal, his crime being, not murder but failure to resist the untrammelled passion of gold. The world of *The Jew of Malta* appears to be as such wherein A. Comte's "religion of humanity" that "lent humanism its non or anti-christian flavour" is replaced by religion of wealth—wealth alone is held in high esteem. The Jew is a great mercantile power in Malta, he does not indulge in fanciful imaginations. He is a man of action and one, who cannot see a false being played upon him and cannot counteract, is doomed. M.M. Mahood rightly observed that Marlowe is "no prophet of a future society"[37] nor one can be but the Mammon-worshipping world of his invention in the play has certainly a ring of prophecy which finds manifestation in the display of much evil in the Elizabethan and Jacobean tragedies.

Why does the Jew not feel himself safe even after Abigail and the two friars of rival orders are put out of the way? It is not that the inner is haunted by imaginary fears, the reality is something outside Machiavellianism. Any obstacles thwarting his aspirations must be pulled down, be they human or non-human. The next victim is, therefore, Ithamore who survives as a witness to his black deeds and he must die. Barabas' resolve to do away with a poor slave for the fault that he has been so faithful to him is symbolic of the clash of interest in a bourgeois society which is the capitalists' struggle against each other.

Barabas, disguised as a French musician, goes to the brothel where he happens to encounter Ithamore. Ithamore is invited by Bellamira, a courtesan of great beauty. There he, tight with drink, blurts out in full details the crimes which he and his master together committed. Barabas carries poisoned flowers in his hat whose smell as per strategy will kill them all. But before the poison begins to work, Bellamira and Pilia-Borza approach the Governor to disclose all about the Jew's black deeds.

BELLA: Governor, hear me speak.
I bring the news by whom thy son was slain:
Mathias did it not; it was the Jew.
PILIA: Who, besides the slaughter of these gentlemen
Poison'd his own daughter and the nuns
Strangled a friar and I know not what
Mischief beside.[38]

The revelation is repulsive and nauseating. The Governor asks his men to remove the Jew away because his "sight is death to me". But the Jew stands dauntless and addresses the people of Malta in a heroic vein to demand justice, not to Ferneze, which is a part of policy to win mass sympathy.

You men of Malta, hear me speak.
She is a courtesan, and he a thief,
And he my bondman; let me have law,
For none of this can prejudice my life.[39]

After the removal from the scene, the Jew rises from the supposed stupor of death which is, in Hunter's words, "a parody of resurrection"[40] but his death would mean the death of the play and, moreover, the dramatist has perhaps something more to project with Barabas as alive which fits into the moral scale of the play; how evil ultimately comes to ruination.

BARA: (rising) What, all alone? Well fare, sleepy drink!
I'll be reveng'd on this accursed town;
For by my means Calymath shall enter in
I'll help to slay their children and their wives,
To fire the churches, pull their houses down,
Take my goods too, and seize upon my lands.
I hope to see the Governor a slave,
And, rowing in a gallery, whipt to death.[41]

The soliloquy is a brilliant piece of comedy but otherwise a fine theatrical aid for our understanding of how things are to go.

The circumstances in which Barabas is discovered in this posture are mystifying, though someone may dismiss the episode as melodramatic. Barabas is very naturally taken as a spy and with it the action becomes more intriguing to create the truth of the whole situation in which the Machiavellian power-play comes to the fore—policy cutting into policy. Calymath ironically falls into the Jew's confidence when he explains to him the details of the seizure of Malta which otherwise is a hard challenge. Calymath is aware of the wrongs inflicted on him by the Christians. The Jew explains to him the subtleties of his stratagem. He says that he will enter with the five hundred soldiers into the heart of the city through a tunnel (the sewer) dug out in a hollow rock for "running streams" of the city and will rise with them in the middle of the town to open the gates for "you to enter in" when he attacks the walls with the rest of the soldiers. The flawless scheme, so ingenuously structured, generates optimism, the seizure seems to be within sight, the reward is Jew's elevation to the post of the Governor of Malta. The pact is sealed by a brilliant speech pattern which is a stamp of Marlowe's poetic power.

> CALY: If this be true, I'll make thee Governor.
>
> BARA: And if it be not true, then let me die.[42]

The plot is not a product of a simple mind, it is a creation of the black twisted brain symbolizing the serpentine thought-process, fraught with undertones of irony. Harry Levin also uses the word 'serpent' in the sub-title "more of the serpent" for Barabas in his study of *The Jew of Malta*.

The plot works as it is constructed. Ferneze and the Maltese are made captives and left to the mercy of the Jew, the new Governor of Malta. But he is not a naive to be seduced by such trifling honours. He is fully aware of the predicament of a Jew among the Christians and thus harbours no illusion. He is very much pragmatic in the sense that he resolves to be firm in the new post, keeping in view the urgency of the doctrine of self-preservation as put forth by Machiavelli in *The Prince*. It is nobody's friendship he is interested in, the truth is that he is friendly with one from whom, he thinks, he can siphon the maximum material profits. It is not the political power either that he can relish. If it had been so he would not have decided to sell back the post of Governorship to Ferneze in the exchange of money. There is hardly any move which is not animated by the chemistry of the materialistic world-outlook. He says,

> Thus, loving neither, will I live with both,
> Making a profit of my policy;
> And he from whom my most advantage comes,
> Shall be my friend.[43]

That is why after the seizure of Malta, the fugitive Governor sees the possibility of gaining huge sums from the Maltese if Calymath is destroyed. The whole thing fits well into his Machiavellian policy that if the purse swells, so does the power. His mind moves with utmost swiftness from one situation to another but it cannot be simply dismissed as whimsicality or freakishness. Rather, it is the very strategy of survival he keeps evolving by choice without ever being conscious of its tragic implications that it might come to boomerang on him. His somersaults have psychological implications: the threat to his economic empire to which he so tenaciously clings.

Nevertheless, in order to translate the idea of acquisition of gold into reality and see his policies bear fruits, the Jew sends for Ferneze and shares with him the deal of dissolution of the slavery of Malta. He explains how Calymath is to be surrendered by fraud to the Maltese Knights and his soldiers are to be destroyed in the nunnery, standing as an outhouse to the city by way of explosion. One can say that the alliance of the Jew and the Christians against the Turks is a show of Machiavellian opportunism which is partly true. But there is something more. The glare of gold has paralyzed the vision to the extent that he cannot see the evident fear of jointing hands with a fallen enemy. It is the Jew who is largely responsible for the debacle of Malta. Ferneze might be in search of an opportunity to hit him back and, therefore, in the existing situation, the Jew's offer is a tactical error. Ferneze has seen the free play of the Jew's devastating powers to set things right and thus he has no vital ground to be sceptical about the success of freeing Malta "now remediless". It is true that at the centre of each episode it is the inordinate lust of gold that animates its spirit but it needs the superhuman and marvellous energy that the Jew has in abundance in him to turn the rat-race urge into a rewarding venture.

Ferneze is also aware of this Jew's weakness for gold. Hence, he promises for a handsome reward and also the gubernatorial status.

> Great sums of money for thy recompense:
>
> Nay, more, do this, and live thou Governor still.[44]

Calymath and his bassoes, as per plotting, are to be feasted in the citadel and his soldiers in a monastery outside the town. Preparations are made for the monastery to be blown up with gun powder and in the citadel, the Jew himself is seen working with a hammer with the carpenters to make a 'dainty gallery' the floor of which is tied with a cable. It is the devil's work because with the cutting of the cable, it would give in, resulting in the destruction of those feasting on it. When the work is over to his satisfaction, the carpenters are richly rewarded with gold. But since the construction of the gallery is a part of policy, he fears its secret be out any moment and thus he offers the innocent carpenters poisoned wine to put a stop to it.

> There, carpenters, divide that gold amongst you.
>
> (Giving money).
>
> Go, swill in bowls of sack and muscadine;
>
> Down to the cellar, taste of all my wines.[45]

The moment when the Turkish Prince ascends the homely stairs of the gallery, someone is to cut the cord and the entire platform will fall asunder in a deep hollow pit leaving no one to survive. Surprisingly enough, the job of cutting the cable is assigned to Ferneze in good faith with the direction as to when he is to cut the cord. Since the strength of the play lies in plot and counterplot, Ferneze sees a good opportunity of doing away with the Jew in this episode by cutting the cable when he (the Jew) himself is alone on the gallery. The amount which Ferneze brings is a 'hundred thousand pounds' which the Jew accepts showing magnanimity that he would take it when the work is done. He appears on the gallery which swings like a scaffold, ready to devour its victim. When he asks Calymath and his followers to ascend the stairs Ferneze comes forward and forbids them to do so saying that he "will shew thee greater courtesy/ Than Barabas would have afforded thee". A shot is sounded within, Ferneze cuts the cord and the gallery gives way. Confusion prevails.

> CALY: How now! What means this?
>
> BARA: Help, help me, Christians, help!
>
> FERN: See, Calymath! This was devis'd for thee.
>
> CALY: Treason, treason! Bassoes, fly![46]

The Jew falls down in a boiling cauldron underneath which is set for Calymath to fall into and roast alive. The wheel of Fortune has taken full circle, it is Ferneze who in place of the Jew holds the cable of Malta's destiny, not even the gods. One is right to say that it is the triumph of Machiavel at the end.

The ambiguity in the Prologue is resolved. What is pertinent is that the spirit of Machiavelli does preside over the play but whether it is manifest in Barabas or Ferneze is no longer a point of debate. The two birds are killed with one stone: the Jew is destroyed and with Calymath's captivity Malta is freed. F. Boas points out that all Marlowe's protagonists are haunting figures in their death which adds strength to the moral scale of the play's argument. Lying in the boiling cauldron the Jew is boasting of his cruel deeds as if he still dreams of towering over the enemy.

> Know, Governor, 'twas I that slew thy son,
> I fram'd the challenge that did make them meet.
> Know, Calymath, I aim'd thy overthrow:
> And, Had I but escap'd this stratagem,
> I would have brought confusion on you all,
> Damn'd Christians, dogs, and Turkish infidels![47]

And with a last agonized cry "Die, life! Fly, soul! Tongue, curse thy fill, and die". Barabas's game of 'Realpolitik' ends. He accepts defeat with a resolution as Tamburlaine accepted his own with calmness of mind. The Jew's plot is unearthed, Calymath is saved but with the blasting of the monastery, his soldiers are massacred. Calymath is much shaken by the suddenness of this overthrow. Ferneze interprets this Jew's monstrous treason as magnanimity. The sarcastic barb is evident.

> A Jew's courtesy.
> For he that did by treason work our fall,
> By treason hath deliver'd thee to us.[48]

Calymath as captive is allowed to return to Ottoman only after the loss done to Malta is repaired.

> Know, therefore, till thy father hath made good
> The ruins done to Malta and to us,
> Thou canst not part; for Malta shall be freed,
> Or Selim ne'er return to Ottoman.[49]

But there is something more in his overthrow which is the ultimate supremacy of the Maltese over their enemies. F. Boas has pointed out that the last words of the Christian Governor "sound like England's defiant challenge from her sea-girt shores to all enemies in the immediate post-Armada years".[50]

The first play of Tamburlaine ends in glory and triumph, the second in death but in death there is a note of praise that the words on epitaph tell that the man was the pride of earth and heaven. What of Barabas? What is the metaphysics of decline from the sword power of Tamburlaine to money power of the Jew? To reject his lustfulness for gold would mean to ignore the whole Renaissance world-outlook. What is the psychology of his crimes that his money power keeps cutting across the Christians and the non-Christians alike? His ruthless conduct against the Christians could be a part of his racial hatred but what of those who are not Christians and even after they are destroyed in wantonness like flies? Is Abigail's conversion so heinous a crime as could be set right only by poison? Mathias, Lodovick, the two Friars, Barnardine and Jacomo, the trio, 'Bellamira—Pillia Borja—Ithamore', the carpenters, the five hundred Turkish soldiers—all are removed from his way as if they were obstacles to his plotting. The graph of his crime, one can say, is melodramatic, but its human appeal cannot be undervalued.

The real genesis of Barabas's tragic doom are, therefore, the moral inadequacies as prompted by false humanism and his failure to put undercheck the dragon of covetousness and dishonest business dealings—'a hundred for hundred' to raise his power in a hostile universe wherein there is no intervention of gods, the God that he invokes is money god—the loyalty of which, ironically, drives him to a boiling cauldron, symbolic of the sea of lust of mercantilism that drowned Eliot's Phonecian sailor, Phelebas. The play's philosophy is thus simple; collecting wealth is no sin provided it is not put to disuse. What humanizes the natural/savage man are the spiritual concerns which, when usurped by the commercial greed and hysteria of anthropocentricism, leave man dehumanized to the point of the loss of the being and the denial of all bonds of humanity. The unnatural violent deaths, including that of this own daughter, are the black deeds of one who has sold out his soul to the devil. And, therefore, such a man, be he Machiavellian or not, does not fit into the moral scheme of the dramatist and is destined to doom.

NOTES

1. "In his selection of a name there is a deeper significance, for Barabas was the criminal whom the Jews preferred to Jesus, when Pilate offered to release a prisoner. One of the witnesses against Marlowe's Atheism, Richard Baines, quotes his assertion: 'That Christ deserved better to die then Barabas and that the Jews made a good Choice, though Barabas were both a thief and a murtherer'. It could also be said that, if Christ died for all men, he died most immediately for Barabas; and that Barabas was the man whose mundane existence profited most immediately from Christ's sacrifice." (Harry Levin, *Christopher Marlowe: The Overreacher*, p. 84.)
2. After Venice, Antwerp became the point to connect the East and the West, but when it was plundered by the Spaniards, the centre of trade between the East and the West was shifted to London.
3. *Faust, Part One*, trans. Philip Wayne, London: Penguin Books Ltd., 1949, p. 91.
4. Quoted in Georg Lukacs *Goethe and His Age*, London: Merlin Press, 1979, p. 198.

   "What exists for me through the medium of money, what I can pay for, i.e. what money can buy, is what I am as the possessor of the money. The properties of the money are my own (its possessor's) properties and essential powers. What I am and can do is, then, not all determined by my individuality. I am ugly, but I can buy myself the most beautiful woman. Hence, I am not ugly, for the effect of ugliness, its power to repel, is nullified by money. In my individuality I am lame, but money provides me with twenty-four legs, hence, I am not lame. I am a wicked, dishonest, unscrupulous, dull-witted man, but money is honoured and so too is its possessor. Money is the highest good, so its possessor is good. Besides, money saves me the trouble of being dishonest; hence, I am presumed honest. I am dull-witted, but since money is the real spirit of all things, how could its possessor be dull-witted? Moreover, he can buy himself clever people, and is not he who has power over the clever more clever than they? I who can possess, by means of money, everything for which the human heart longs, do I not possess all human capacities? Does not my money, therefore, transform all incapacities into their opposite?"

5. Ben Jonson, *Volpone: Or the Fox*, ed. by David Cook, London: Metheun and Co. Ltd., 1967, p. 61.
6. Prologue to *The Jew of Malta*, J.B. Steane (ed.), *Christopher Marlowe: The Complete Plays*, London, Penguin Books, 1969, p. 349.
7. *The Jew of Malta*, p. 349.
8. *Ibid.*, p. 352.
9. *Ibid.*, p. 350.
10. *Ibid.*, p. 358.
11. *Ibid.*, p. 363.
12. *Ibid.*, p. 368.
13. *Idem.*
14. *Ibid.*, p. 369.
15. *Ibid.*, p. 359.
16. Hasidism was a religious sect founded in Poland in the 18th century. It became popular among the east European Jewish community. It is characterized by an emphasis on mysticism, prayer, religious zeal and fellow feelings. It shows concern not for self but for others.
17. *Ibid.*, p. 378.
18. Idem.
19. *Ibid.*, p. 379.
20. *Idem.*
21. *Idem.*
22. *Ibid.*, p. 389.
23. *Idem.*
24. *Ibid.*, p. 390.
25. E.M.W. Tillyard in *The Elizabethan World Picture* has shown how the Elizabethans maintained the medieval concept of man, a being of dual nature standing "at the apex

of Nature's pyramid with one foot upon the angelic nature". (M.M. Mahood, *Poetry and Humanism*, p. 14.)

26. *Ibid.*, p. 391.
27. *Idem.*
28. *Idem.*
29. *Ibid.*, p. 392.
30. *Ibid.*, p. 399.
31. *Ibid.*, p. 400.
32. Wilbur Sanders, *The Dramatist and the Received Idea*, Cambridge: Cambridge University Press, 1968, p. 45.
33. *The Jew of Malta*, pp. 400-01.
34. *Ibid.*, p. 401.
35. *Ibid.*, p. 404.
36. *Ibid.*, p. 405.
37. M.M. Mahood, *Poetry and Humanism*, p. 81.
38. *The Jew of Malta*, pp. 416-17.
39. *Ibid.*, p. 417.
40. G.K. Hunter, "The Theology and Marlowe's *The Jew of Malta*, in *Journal of Warourg and Courtauld Institute*, No. 7, 1964, p. 233.
41. *The Jew of Malta*, pp. 418-19.
42. *Ibid.*, p. 419.
43. *Ibid.*, p. 423.
44. *Ibid.*, p. 422.
45. *Ibid.*, p. 426.
46. *Ibid.*, p. 428.
47. *Ibid.*, pp. 428-29.
48. *Ibid.*, p. 429.
49. *Ibid.*, pp. 429-30.
50. F. Boas, *Christopher Marlowe*, p. 147.

6

Edward II

As Marlowe chose a wandering Jew the hero of the play to satirize the evil consequences of the worship of sham gods, so the singularity of the choice of presenting a period of the British history on the stage is made, keeping in view the same factor to study man in relation to time's disorders, be he a commoner or a royal personage. It is true that since the defeat of the Spanish Armada no theme was more popular on the stage than that of the British history but Marlowe's choice of the period of Edward's reign (1307-27) is for the reason that it fully fits into a perfect tragic formula: a serious defect in the character of the hero which is the ruinous passion, first for Piers Gaveston,[1] the French, then for the Spensers, the English and the ensuing conflict between the king and the barons, the king's momentary victory and the ultimate defeat and death. Unlike the earlier heroes who strive for power, Edward is a king who already wields power but power abused which renders him a weakling, "a Mycetes in the throne of Tamburlaine". Though Edward is at the centre of the action of the play, yet unlike the other plays, being one-man tragedy, here the interest is spread over other characters also and thus the play is as much a tragedy of Edward as of Queen Isabella and Mortimer. Marlowe closely follows the source material to vivify the king's account and if there are deviations in the portrayal of certain characters (for example, Isabella's delineation is for the most part imaginary) it is a part of the dramatic necessity.

Holinshed, shows Edward "passing his time in voluptuous pleasure and riotous excess", his court "furnished with companies of jesters, ruffians, flattering parasites, musicians and other vile and naughtie ribalds", the king is reported to have spent days and night in "jesting, pla'eing, blanketing and in such other filthie and dishonourable exercises". Thus, the presentation of conduct of a voluptuary king is in accord with the spirit of the age because a king too happens to be human and it is very unlikely to imagine that nobility is not susceptible to human frailty or when calamity befalls a conspicuous person, it is the design of an inscrutable fate.

Tragedy, as Marlowe holds, is not a thing of kings and princes alone but a matter of individual heroes and one's world outlook is not characterized by rank or station but by the degree of awareness of his humanity to fully realize himself in face of the obstacles to its fulfillment. Sovereignty is not something to be conferred on man, what makes a man king are kingly virtues such as valour, heroism, nobility of heart, wisdom to rule and not the crown or the gilded attires. The balance between the two extremes, the medieval and the modern, should remain unbroken so as to keep under check the excessive fondness for 'shows' and festivities, lust for appetite and beauty that renders a king subject to indignities to the degree which human imagination can hardly conceive of. After Gaveston's removal Edward cries "Was ever a king thus overruled as I?" Is the crying moral? Or how can we reconcile the stupidity of a sovereign head, limited to measuring power in terms of protecting the interest of an individual rather than that of the state? How strange that one, who himself is responsible for destroying the Elizabethan idea of order and orthodoxy, questions the morality of what others do!

It was the time when the loyalty to the Queen and the spirit of nationalism were of paramount interest and thus a rebellion was something unheard of. But it is otherwise a matter of concern too as to what makes the barons rebel against the crown. Agreed that the nobility could be haughty and arrogant but how to condone Edward's utter neglect of the obligations to self and the state and his infatuation for Gaveston? The setting tends to be contrary to the spirit of humanism and conventionality, the play probes deeper into the complexities of the perversion of human relations, arising out of the changing value-orientation of the 16th century English society.

The play's opening is at once arresting. The tragic flaw is introduced in the person of Gaveston who appears reading a letter in the street which Edward wrote to recall him from the exile: the words "share the kingdom of thy dearest friend" are by no means a mystification of the identity of the friend and the bond of friendship existing between the two. But when the clandestine designs of this (friend?) who is very much anxious to run into king's arms find tongue in a soliloquy, the fog begins to settle down.

> I must have wanton poets, pleasant wits,
> Musicians, that with touching of a string
> May draw the plaint king which way I please.
> Music and poetry is his delight;
> Therefore I'll have Italian masques by night,
> Sweet speeches, comedies, and pleasing shows;
> And in the day, when he shall walk abroad,
> Like sylvan nymphs my pages shall be clad;
> My men, like satyrs grazing on the lawns,
> Shall with their goat-feet dance an antic hay;
> Sometimes a lovely boy in Dian's shape,
> With hair that gilds the water as it glides,
> Crownets of pearl about his naked arms,
> And in his sportful hands an olive tree,
> To hide those parts which men delight to see,
> Shall bathe him in a spring; and there, hard by,
> One like Actaeon, peeping through the grove
> Shall by the angry goddess be transform'd,
> And running in the likeness of an hart
> By yelping hounds pull'd down, and seem to die;
> Such things as these best please his majesty.[2]

The soliloquy is marked by the lust of the eye and paganism the Renaissance temper delighted in. Nothing is kept obscure. We learn about Gaveston's stratagem to freely exploit Edward's homosexuality and gullibility for his own advantage. The classical myths and legends in Marlowe assume particular significance, they are employed as a powerful aid to reflect the truth of man. The Actaeon-myth[3] is one such myth that carries within it the seeds of decay and moral degeneration to bring into focus the hero's predicament and what is to the seen is whether he escapes the hunter's fate, while feasting his eye on the sights forbidden to man. We feel much shocked to learn that if the things are to go off the way as Gaveston proposes to set, the stately ship is sure to sink, Gaveston is well aware of the king's moral inadequacies and thus the planting of the boys, dressed as classical nymphs/deities in his way, is a well-orchestrated feat of Machiavellianism to tighten his hold on a weakling which is suggested by the line "May draw the pliant king which way I please". Here is a hint of the king's helplessness, born of wantonness and homosexual escapades.

It is partly through the device of the letter and partly through the portentous antagonism between the king and the nobles that Marlowe creates a situation which is characteristic of an expressionistic play. Lancaster, the two Mortimers, Warwick express their displeasure and contempt over the Gaveston-issue. To Elder Mortimer's candid proclamation "If you love us, my lord, hate Gaveston", Edward's resolution, "I'll have my will" is ill-conceived in that the word 'will' in Elizabethan sense suggests authoritarianism and individualism which are against the humanist spirit of devotion to common humanity. Humanism is an attempt to understand life and the world, it "is a moral conviction" but Edward does not seem to have trust in its appeal. When the Earl of Kent, the king's half-brother, rebukes the nobles for their display of a conduct of ancestral arrogance and impudence, the Younger Mortimer loses patience and speaks of the sword power in Tamburlainian vein which adds to the king's weakness and throws a hint how events may take a turn,

Come, let us leave the brain-sick king.
And henceforth parley with our naked swords.[4]

Even Lancaster threatens in the same vein. He warns the king of the impending disaster and the possibility of the throne floating in a sea of blood.

Adieu, my lord; and either change your mind,
Or look to see the throne, where you should sit,
To float in blood, and at thy wanton head
The glozing head of thy base minion thrown.[5]

It is not that the nobility is all arrogant and drugged by class-pride, there is some element of sanity in what they suggest. And if Edward follows their advice that would mean Gaveston's exile but then, one can say, that would also mean the death of the play which is also true. Edward could have easily had his will and silenced the nobles but the manner in which he stands against them to defend Gaveston is a demonstration of irresponsible bohemianism and thus he looks a ridiculous figure. After the departure of the nobles, Edward dramatically becomes conscious of his sovereignty and instead of seeking reconciliation to ease the crisis threatens war to have his 'will', placing a 'minion' against the value of living.

Brother, display my ensigns in the field:
I'll bandy with the barons and the earls,
And either die, or live with Gaveston.[6]

Tamburlaine seeks the expansion of self through the expansion of empire by sword power, Edward does not do so. It is not exaggeration to say that Tamburlaine is cast in a young man's vision of greatness in action, Edward "is blankly deadened, a sucked orange". And this is one factor why in the projection of the image of man there are varying trends in Marlowe-criticism. Eugene Waith has made a very apt comparison between Tamburlaine and *Edward II* in regard to what actually happens. "When *Tamburlaine* seems to open up even wider prospectus upto the moment of the hero's death, *Edward II* closes down until the focus is upon a prison, a death bed, a bier". As a king, Edward has no need to seek power, he has it already thrust upon him which, as voluptuary, he wants to enjoy and thus prefers the amorous fulfillment to military victory.

Gaveston's reaction to what goes off on the stage between Edward and the nobles is a sufficient hint about the events to follow. However, after the exeunt of the nobles, Gaveston comes forward and makes his physical appearance. Edward stands as if arrested by spell and, being oblivious of his sovereignty, grows passionate to embrace Gaveston saying,

> What, Gaveston! Welcome! kiss not my hand:
> Embrance me, Gaveston, as I do thee.
> Why shouldst thou kneel? know'st thou not who I am?
> Thy friend, thyself, another Gaveston!
> Not Hylas was more mourned of Hercules
> Than thou has been of me since thy exile.[7]

The fanciful meeting of the two lovers is the prelude of the ironic wish-fulfillment which at once brings into focus the singularity of their relationship as suggested by the "Hylas-Hercules" imagery. Gaveston like a cunning politician uses, in theological terms, the image of a condemned soul in purgatory to explain the torment that he suffered in exile which is fraught with touches of hypocrisy and opportunism. He says,

> And since I went from hence, no soul in hell
> Hath felt more torment than poor Gaveston.

Kent also warns Edward to be temperate in his conduct with the 'minion' but he turns impervious to such a well-meaning advice which is a sure sign of a fractured vision and lack of judgement. Edward showers titles and offices upon Gaveston indiscriminately without looking at its ironic implication that it would amount to injuring the merit of the nobility. Gaveston is made Lord High Chamberlain, Chief Secretary to the state and to the King and Earl of Cornwall, King and Lord of Man. And feeling that Gaveston's worth is far above his gifts, he places the guard and treasury at his disposal and even the 'seal'. Thus, Gaveston is virtually a replacement of the king's sovereignty and the power associated with it, and with it the stage is set for his tragedy.

If for these dignities thou be envied,
I'll give thee more; for, but to honour thee,
Is Edward pleas'd with kingly regiment.
Fear'st thou thy person? Thou shall have a guard:
Wantest thou gold? go to my treasury:
Wouldst thou be lov'd and fear'd? receive my seal
Save or condemn, and in our name command
What so thy mind affects, or fancy likes.[8]

Gaveston's hypocrisy and guile come on the fore in a classical parallel: so heavily laden with titles and honours he imagines himself as if Caesar himself were riding in a triumphant procession through the streets of Rome. Marlowe thus creates in him a streak of hubris and ambition, in addition to moral perversion and lustfulness to assure his fall.

It shall suffice me to enjoy your love;
Which whiles I have, I think myself as great
As Ceasar riding in the Roman street.
With captive kings at his triumphant car.[9]

Gaveston rides high on the power of gold in the treasury, the very seal and the honours conferred on him which are the 'waxen wings' which will melt away with soaring high beyond limitations. The Phaeton-image,[10] signifying the fall of man on way of hubris, is central in Marlowe of which Gaveston is a powerful extension. The hostility between the crown and the church and the struggle for supremacy between the two became more prominent after the Church of England got separated from the Roman Church during the reign of Henry VIII. And the treatment meted out to the Bishop of Coventry who procured Gaveston's banishment is a tactical error. His material resources, goods and house all are given to Gaveston and he is thrown into the Tower. The attack on the clergy is morally reprehensible, Edward fails to measure the power of the church, being greater than that of the peers.

The Archbishop of Canterbury is intimated of the foul assault on the clergy. At his advice the barons assemble at the New Castle to sign a decree of Gaveston's instant banishment. Edward plays trick upon the barons to placate their anger by offering high offices and in case of discontentment, he is willing to have the nation divided into several kingdoms for them to rule and himself offer to retire "to frolic with my dearest Gaveston" into some secluded corner. What a show of farcical resolution!

As Faustus suffers the intellectual decline under the effect of unholy practices, so it is the impact of homoeroticism that has totally destroyed the power of 'seeing' in Edward: he feels it is Gaveston alone who loves him. To Mortimer's question— "Why should you love him whom the world hates", Edward's reply that "Because he loves me more than all the world" is an attempt "to fortify his shaky self-esteem". But Edward is unaware of its ironic implications that such an expression of possessiveness, to the exclusion of other relations, would rouse jealousy and bring schism between him and the queen. How comical that he turns to a French without ever being sure of it whether his love is a pose of Machiavellian opportunism or sincere expression of emotional ties that true friendship entails!

The Archbishop impresses upon Edward's mind the precariousness of the situation and the political disaster involved in this act of moral effrontery. Edward is otherwise not blind to the power of Papal authority and thus fearing the threat of excommunication signs the decree desperately saying "Instead of ink I'll write it with my tears". The peers and the Archbishop feel at ease and hurry forth to see that the decree is enforced. After their departure, Edward is left alone on the stage. Overwhelmed by preposterous sentimentalism, he likens himself with a hounded lion under the tryanny of the two authorities—the church and the nobility. The anger finds expression in an anti-Papal tirade in a soliloquy

Proud Rome, that hatchest such imperial grooms,
For these thy superstitious taper-lights,
Wherewith thy antichristian churches blaze,

I'll fire thy crazed buildings, and enforce
The papal towers to kill the lowly ground.[11]

the one,[12] similar to that we have in *The Massacre of Paris*.

Edward is conscious of the magic power associated with the crown which is no doubt his pragmatism and down-to-earth attitude to reality. He asks Gaveston to "go or I shall be deposed". The choice of the crown is saner but it is tainted by random flashes of weakness of passion. He consoles the 'minion' with soothing words and promises that "my love shall never decline". And he will have a hasty revenge upon the conspirators, "But I will reign to be revenged of them". Gaveston is appointed the Governor of Ireland. His laconic utterance "It is something to be pitted of a king" is a creation of a diabolic mind to impress on Edward that a king is not to be rendered so powerless and impotent. But it is also distrust that ambition generates. Instead of advising the king to seek reconciliation Gaveston wants him to be resolute in dealing with the peers which is a display of cynical opportunism and unfeeling conduct in moments of crisis.

Marlowe brings in another victim of Edward's hedonistic temper who is queen Isabella herself at this critical juncture and with it the crisis deepens and the queen's conduct comes as much within the moral range of the dramatist as of Edward's. The very sight of Isabella ignites the ember in the ashes and both Edward and his favourite indulge in throwing unsavoury moral accusations against her. To her question "Whither goes my lord?", Edward's reply is wholly unkingly and treacherous.

KING EDWARD: Fawn not on me, French strumpet, get thee gone!

QUEEN ISABELLA: On whom but on my husband should I fawn?

GAVESTON: On Mortimer, with whom, ungentle Queen.

I say no more-judge you the rest my lord.

QUEEN ISABELLA: In saying this, thou wrong's me, Gaveston

Is't not enough that thou corrupt'st my lord,

And art a bawd to his affections

But thou must call mine honour thus in question?

GAVESTON: I mean not so; your grace must pardon me

EDWARD: Thou art too familiar with that Mortimer,

And by thy means is Gaveston exil'd

But I would wish thee reconcile the lords.

Or thou shalt ne'er be reconcil'd to me.[13]

Gaveston is critical of Isabella's morals in the presence of Edward who himself, in place of protecting her honour, calls her a "French strumpet" to humour his French favourite. The dubious threat of reconciliation renders Isabella orphaned and helpless. She thinks of fleeing to the forest to live like a recluse in seclusion. She says that she can bear Gaveston but cannot see the king "oppressed by civil mutinies" which is a reflection of her essential nobility of conduct. And, therefore, in the existing situation, if she turns to Mortitmer, who is then responsible for turning her into a demoniacal force? Gaveston is Edward's Mephistophilis whose pernicious moral impact has alienated the king from nobility, the court and from his own self, it is Edward's persistently spurning of a loving and virtuous queen that finally drives her to Mortimer as a mistress. And for her rallying the force later in the second half of the play against Edward, it is said that she holds the destiny of the play which is not wholly true. The acceptance of such a view would mean to miss the dramatic significance of the, 'Gaveston-theme' which is at the centre of the play. As a victim of this "Ganymede-complex" the queen shares Juno's predicament. She knows that Edward will ever keep doting "on Gaveston", and she would remain "for ever miserable".

Like fratic Juno will I fill the earth
With ghastly murmur of my sighs and cries;
For never doted Jove on Ganymede
So much as he on cursed Gaveston
But that will more exasperate his wrath;
I must entreat him, I must speak him fair
And be a means to call home Gaveston
And yet he'll ever dote on Gaveston:
And so am I for ever miserable.[14]

Edward's mind gravitates toward evil, he thinks of exploiting Isabella's intimacy with the barons to have the decree of Gaveston's exile repealed. Isabella somehow succeeds in persuading the Younger Mortimer for having the order of the banishment nullified. Mortimer impresses upon the mind of the peers the dire necessity to recall Gaveston because his stay, as the Governor of Ireland, will be a threat to their soverignty. He explains to them the danger of money power that cuts deeper than the sword power. It is also presumed that perhaps Gaveston after his recall could be considerate to respect the nobility and in case he continues to be wayward and offending then a rebellion is fully justified in the interest of the country as a whole, though it is condemned as a treason against the king. F. Boas's observation in this regard is worth-quoting, "Marlowe may well have had in mind, not only the lords, who reluctantly yield to Mortimer's persuasion, but also Elizabeth's government, which did not welcome the presentation of rebellion on the stage". The barons see a logic in his argument and at last agree to recall Gaveston. Edward feels overjoyed to have his favorite back in his arms. The rewards begin to flow generously, each baron is raised to a high post. His niece whom Gaveston is to marry is also happy to learn of Gaveston's recall.

The scene shifts before Tynemouth Castle where Edward is seen breathlessly waiting for Gaveston's arrival. His mind is so much over-possessed by the thought of Gaveston that an urgent affair of political significance which is the invasion of the king of France in Normandy is dismissed as a 'trifle' with the words "We will expel him when we please?" as reported by the Young Mortimer. Gaveston appears and Edward welcomes him to the royal castle. Marlowe dramatizes the vulgar and the debased show of power of the two bohemians. The problem with Edward is that in the absence of Gaveston he is a different person but at his very sight his imagination runs riot and he behaves otherwise. He desires the barons to recognize Gaveston's powers and salute him which they do but the tone grows highly mordent. This injures Gaveston's pride and on Edward's promptings "Return it to their throats; I'll be thy warrant", he uses a highly insulting language, having a 'Gascon taint'.

Base, leaden earls, that glory in your birth,
Go sit at home, and eat your tenants' beef,
And come not here to scoff at Gaveston
Whose mounting thoughts did never creep so low
As to bestow a look on such as you.[15]

Lancaster and Mortimer are roused into anger. They draw swords. Gavestan is wounded by Mortimer for which he is banished from the court. And Edward makes a hasty departure with a warning which amounts to forcing a senseless war on the nobility.

But, if I live, I'll tread upon their heads
That think with high looks thus to tread me down.
Come, Edmund, let's away and levy men.
'Tis war that must abate these barons' pride.[16]

It so happens that Mortimer Elder is made a captive by the Scots and they demand a ransom of five thousand pounds for his freedom which Edward refuses to sanction and curtly tells Mortimer to ransom his uncle himself. This further widens the growing distrust and hostility between the crown and the barons. Edward lacks that Baconian worldly wisdom to understand the nuances of statecraft policies. He is unaware of the ironic implications of the refusal to ransom war-prisoners which is the moral obligation of the state.

The Younger Mortimer is backed by his peers. His jibe at Edward's soldierliness finds expression in a remarkable piece of poetry which further displumes his kingliness.

> When wert thou in the field with banner spread?
> But once, and then thy soldiers march'd like players,
> With garish robes, not armour; and thyself,
> Bedaub'd with gold, rode laughing at the rest,
> Nodding and shaking of thy spangled crest,
> Where women's favours hung like labels down.[17]

The tirade continues. His description of the court as suggested by the word 'naked' is also a fine exposition of Edward's misgovernance and indifference to stately obligations that destroyed the institution of the peerage and the very piety of the courtly virtues—all good values are supposed to be found in the court but now they are found elsewhere.

> Thy court is naked, being bereft of those
> That make a king seem glorious to the world,
> I mean the peers, whom thou shouldst dearly love.
> Libels are cast against thee in the street;
> Ballads and rhymes made of thy overthrow.[18]

But the king has his way and his will, though perverted. In order to assert his sovereignty, he brings out the essential incompatibility between a lion and the 'cockerels'. What the cockerels have to do before a lion? But the whole thing verges on Popean irony: the small becoming great, the great small.

> How oft have I been baited by these peers,
> And dare not be reveng'd, for their power is great!
> Yet, shall the crowing of these cockerels
> Affright a lion? Edward, unfold thy paws,
> And let their lives' blood slake thy fury's hunger.
> If I be cruel and grow tyrannous,
> Now let them thank themselves, and rue too late.[19]

He makes admission of nobility as power. The whole meaning is centered on the word "If" which suggests weakness rather than power. The resolution to "unfold thy paws" amounts to civil war and thus unfortunate. Kent represents the spirit of true humanism, his intervention at this moment is both moral and obligatory but it is a pity that he too turns a traitor in his eyes when he urges the king to banish Gaveston forever to avert rebellion and restore order in the state.

> KING EDWARD: Traitor, be gone! Whine thou with Mortimer.
>
> KENT: So will I, rather than with Gaveston.
>
> KING EDWARD: Out of my sight, and trouble me no more!
>
> KENT: No marvel though thou scorn thy noble peers
> When I thy brother am rejected thus.[20]

What could Kent do after such an ignoble neglect and disdainful overthrow but join the barons? The peers have laid seize of the Tynemouth Castle and a civil war is imminent for which Edward's folly is wholly responsible and it is so because the intention of the dramatist is perhaps to show his weakness, not strength. Weakness does not act but is acted upon and if it acts, the actions are bound to be ineffective and perverted. This is one factor that in the present play the interest is shifted from the hero over to the other characters and the play is as much a tragedy of Gaveston, Mortimer and Isabella as of Edward who succumbs to one or the other bourgeois evil, like craziness for power, moral perversion, lustfulness, and machiavellian opportunism.

Gaveston is married to the only daughter of Gloucester. The Tynemouth Castle is the haven where Edward is making frolics with Gaveston. What an irony that the castle is besieged by the rebellious barons but Edward cares little of this impending political upheaval!

> What care I though the earls begirt us round?

But before the peers' hands reach Gaveston, Edward suspects the danger and makes his 'minion' ship off to Scarborough. Even in anxiety-ridden moments, Edward's conduct is unkingly in that he bids farewell to Gaveston and the bride but calculatingly ignores even saying a few words of formal courtesy to the queen. On the contrary, he again accuses her of adulterous relations with Mortimer which lowers down his image in our eyes.

KING EDWARD: Farewell, sweet Gaveston; and farewell, nice.

QUEEN ISABELLA: No farewell to poor Isabel thy queen?

KING EDWARD: Yet, yes, for Mortimer your lover's sake.

QUEEN ISABELLA: Heavens can witness, I love none but you.[21]

However, Gaveston is pursued and arrested. What follows thereafter is all history as Holinshed narrates. The presentation of history on the stage needs restructuring and regrouping to create the effect of convincingness which is one requirement of artistic truth. Gaveston is brought as a captive before the barons, he is disarmed. Mortimer ignores him and hurls foul abuses on him to deflate his supposed magnetic spell which, one can say, are an expression of patriotism and love of the crown. But the words have overtones of aristocratic bias and personal prejudices.

Thou proud disturber of thy country's peace,
Corrupter of thy king, cause of these broils,
Base flatterer, yield! And, were it not for shame,
Shame and dishonour to a soldier's name,
Upon my weapon's point here should's thou fall,
And welter in thy gore.[22]

The barons reject Edward's passionate desire to have a last meeting with the favourite who is 'marked to die'. He feels so badly ruffled at Gaveston's arrest and knowing that no ransom can rescue him thinks of 'ransom'. The issue of ransom to free Mortimer Elder from the Scots was a political obligation which he so jocularly rejected and now he is willing to ransom out Gaveston where no public obligation is involved. And when the news that Gaveston is beheaded by Warwick in a trench reaches him, the Younger Spenser terms it as something against "law of arms". The king's expression of agony and a wish to die is unkingly and a travesty of good ruling.

O, shall I speak or shall I sign and die![23]

The Younger Spenser shares the inadequacies the age suffers from. It is the love of power and ambition that turns him blind to the repercussions of the advice he gives to Edward to take arms and not to be temperate in dealing with the pears. He has little realization that such a stance will throw the nation into bloodshed. He plays Edward's infatuation for Gaveston for his own advancement and thus the promptings that the murder be avenged are mischievous and machiavellian.

Advance your standard, Edward in the field,
And march to fire them from their starting-holes.[24]

As such, Edward feels encouraged and raising the sword as a witness to earth and the planets swears revenge.

(Kneeling) By earth, the common mother of us all,
By heaven, and all the moving orbs thereof,
By this right hand, and by my father's sword,
And all the honours 'longing to my crown,
I will have heads, and lives for him, as many
As I have manors, castles, towns, and towers! (Rises)[25]

The tone is certainly Tamburlainean but it lacks the commensurate spirit of valour and heroism that makes a shepherd the monarch of the Eastern world. The gesture of 'kneeling' and 'rising' is less a show of resolute self than of a self caught in confusion that has corroded the spiritual and the philosophical insight which enables man to separate the good from the evil. He takes Gaveston's murder as an assault on his humanity and swears to wreck revenge. There were occasions when Edward, as head of the state, was to act promptly like the assault of the king of France on Normandy which was virtually an assault on the nation's sovereignty and which he let go unheeded dismissing it as 'trifle'. But now he is shaken to the roots. Is Gaveston's death so overwhelming and the cause is really so genuine that the world appears to him to be drab and desolate? It is so because it is all a private affair. And thus at one level the play is a study in the clash between the private and the public which could go parallel provided the territory of the two is honoured.

After Gaveston's execution, Marlowe brings in the Spensers—the father and the son—as the king's new favourites to serve as an extension of Gaveston-theme which shows that the king has learnt nothing from the earlier situation. Second, it was a dramatic problem to treat the Spensers as the object of barons' hostility who happen to be English, not French. But Marlowe skillfully overcomes this problem by placing the Yonger Spenser as a member of the Earl of Gloucester's household which is sufficient to incur the barons' anger. Edward is conscious of the crucial conditions pervading the state but he confers titles on him in a fashion, similar to Gaveston's to have his way and partly to humiliate and abate the barons' inexorable pride.

> Spenser, sweet Spenser, I adopt thee here;
> And merely of our love we do create thee
> Earl of Gloucester and Lord Chamberlain,
> Despite of times, despite of enemies.[26]

Marlowe thus shortens history in order to show Spenser's rise to power who is like Gaveston a "base upstart" in the eyes of the barons. No sooner does Edward appoint him to the vacant office of Lord Chamberlain and creates him Earl of Gloucester, than the barons feel incensed and send a herald for his instant removal. He is, they say,

> a putrifying branch
> That deads the royal vine, whose golden leaves
> Empale your princely head, your diadem,
> Whose brightness such pernicious upstarts dim.

But the manner in which Spenser reacts to the barons' moral exhortations in moments of political instability, "Will they still display their pride?" is certainly is show of arrogance that makes him another Gaveston, the bane of Edward's ruination. Spenser is not Gaveston and if the barons cannot see him near to the power, it is all a play of personal will and desire.

Edward by now has not been able to overcome the grief caused by Gaveston's execution and the baron's threat to cast saway Spenser is a fresh assault on his injured egotism and sovereignty. In retaliation, Edward embraces Spenser in the presence of the herald and asks him to go and tell the barons that he "follows at thy heals" with fire and sword "to chastise them". The threat seems an apparent show of power-hysteria.

The result is the battle of Boroughbridge. The king's armies are victorious, the rebel barons are defeated. Warwick and Lancaster are brought as captives and Edward goes the Tamburlaine's way to avenge Gaveston's murder. It is again a political mistake that he stands so defiantly against nobility to destroy it. Warwick and Lancaster are beheaded, the gentle Pembroke is also put to death and Mortimer is thrown into the Tower which is to serve an ironic prologue to his future troubles. Nowhere do we get any explanation of such acts of irrationality as to why Edward beheaded the two brave peers in exchange of a 'minion' and why Mortimer who is the most outspoken of his enemies is given a further chance of life in the Tower from where he could manage to fly any moment. Clifford Leech rightly points out that perhaps Marlowe wanted "to suggest that Edward was a man incapable for profiting from Fortune's momentary flavours".

In Holinshed, Mortimer is drawn in different colours but after Gaveston's murder Marlowe keeps him in prominence as Edward's most inveterate enemy. He is a votary of individualism who believes that there is nothing that cannot be surmounted. The spirit in him is not so easily tamed and paralysed by the state of captivity that find expression in a soliloquy, glowing with unbounded aspirations.

> What Mortimer! Can ragged stony walls
> Immure thy virtue that aspires to heaven?[27]

He calls Edward "England's scourge", and tells him that he cannot be so easily tamed, his "hope surmounts his fortune far".

However, what offends our moral sense is the streak of ambivalence in Mortimer's conduct. He exploits nobility to serve his ends but is not willing to go by its moral code. It is sad that a destructive civil war is thurst upon the innocent people for no fault of their own. Edward grows much impatient to meet the traitors in the battlefield and invokes Phoebus to hasten its course for the night to follow.

Gallop apace, bright Phoebus, through the sky;
And, dusky Night, in rusty iron car,
Between you both shorten the time, I pray,
That I may see that most desired day,
When we may meet these traitors in the field![28]

Mortimer, after his escape from the Tower, joins the queen. She welcomes all her friends and the countrymen who have joined her in the fight against the crown. Her address to justify the revolt by accusing Edward of misgovernance and looseness of morals is highly diplomatic. She says she is not happy to see her countrymen slaughtering each other in "civil broils" but circumstances have made it so.

But what's the help?
Misgovern'd kings are cause of all this wrack;
And, Edward, thou art one among them all,
Whose looseness hath betray'd thy land to spoil,
And made the channels overflow with blood
Of thine own people.[29]

Sensing the queen growing 'overstrong' and the threat of the pursuers Baldock and Spenser advise Edward to fly to some harbour. Their plan to sail to Ireland is thwarted by temptuous winds and they are forced to take refuge in a monastery, the Abbey of Neath. The pursuers happen to reach there and the three are discovered in disguise. Baldock and Spenser are arrested on charge of treason in the queen's order and are taken away. Edward is left lonely. The parting is painful. Edward invokes the stars "O my stars/ Why do you lour unkindly on a king" but the tone is certainly not of unbelief. He has seen power slipping from his fingers. Spenser interprets it as the doing of "angry heavens", but he sees no hand of gods in his down fall, "The gentle heavens have not to do in this" which amounts to accepting his own role in the creation of disaster befalling him. This is the beginning of peripeteia, in Aristotelian sense, essential for the tragic hero.

Edward is brought to the Killingworth Castle as a prisoner where begins the fateful journey to death. By now, he as a king was left never lonely, he was surrounded by the courtiers and the favourites at one or the other time. But henceforth he has to wage a lonely battle for survival against a world which, in the words of F.P. Wilson, "is an altogether grimmer world into which Marlowe takes us, a world of evil and corruption, deeper and darker than that of *Richard II*".[30] The interplay of thoughts and emotions rising in Edward's mind is a complex phenomenon but Marlowe has a good understanding of and insight into the pshychology of defeat and thus he has projected them as realistically as they are true to nature. Barabas' apple cart was upset and he was caught unaware by the enemy for his failure to see that the usurper could also be a usurped any time. But in case of Edward the tragedy is foredoomed.

Marlowe was passionately a moral being and had no taste for the macabre. But the treatment meted out to Edward is a fine exposition of the truth of man who remains a dragon unless moral sense prevails. What happens to Edward in the Kenilworth Castle is equally a show of naked barbaric primitivism. The lamentations and wailings add to the horror which is not made manifest on the stage in the physical form, the enemies are never brought face to face. The fear of their monstrous cruelties haunt his mind, he fears even the safety of his own son. To Leicester's words of comfort, "Be patient, good my lord, cease to lament", Marlowe devotes 34 lines to reflect the varying tone and the mood of the king which is sometimes of regret and self scrutiny, at other times it is of anger, helplessness and wholesale condemnation of laissez-faire in morals. The queen turns "unnatural and false Isabel" in his eyes for throwing him into the state of captivity. He gains realization that words cannot replace deeds. Leicester's comforting and kind words, he knows, will not ease his sorrows as he happens to be a king.

The griefs of private men are soon allay'd:
But not of king. The forest deer, being struck,
Runs to an herb that closeth up the wounds;
But when the imperial lion's flesh is gor'd.
His rends and tears it with his wrathful paw,
(And), highly scorning that the lowly earth
Should drink his blood, mounts up into the air.[31]

The imagery of 'lion' is repeated to suggest the rise of consciousness of sovereignty but little is done to sustain its image. The truth is that it is not a crown but virtues which can keep its halo intact and save the self from disintegration. Edward does nothing but wailing over the change that has stalked him. The thought of Isabella's infamy and moral violence and the nobles, being the rulers, aggravates the tragic gloom.

My nobles rule; I bear the name of king,
I wear the crown; but am controll'd by them,
By Mortimer, and my unconstant queen,
Who spots my nuptial bed with infamy,
Whilst I am lodg'd within this cave of care,
Where sorrow at my elbow still attends,
To company my heart with sad laments,
That bleeds within me for this strange exchange.[32]

As per understanding between the two Machiavels-Mortimer and Isabella, Prince Edward is to be crowned as the king of England and Mortimer appointed the Lord Protector. By doing so, they can easily do away with the king who, it is feared, can slip out of the captivity any time with the support of his followers and again come to power. In order to throw over it the colour of legality, they send the Bishop of Winchester, a man of the church, to demand the crown. When Edward stays stubborn, he is told that the delay and refusal would damage the cause of his son's lawful right to the throne. However, there is a great poignancy in the act of relinquishing the crown, the king is well aware of the plight of a crownless king. He fears that they would crown Mortimer, the king of England and not Prince Edward who is a lamb in the midst of the wolves ready to abridge his life in a moment. He wishes that if Mortimer wear the crown it be transformed into "a blaze of quenchless fire!/ or like the snaky wreaths of Tisiphone".[33]

The exhausting struggle between reason and passion makes the 'abdication scene' highly tragic. He sees in a vision the mysterious figures rise from nowhere, the source of which is his own feverish imagination.

> Inhuman creatures, nurs'd with tiger's milk,
> Why gape you for your sovereign's overthrow?
> My diadem, I mean, and guiltless life.
> See, monsters, see! I'll wear my crown again.[34]

And saying thus he puts on the crown and imagining the power having returned to him, he feels he is a different man and dares to ask them in an authoritarian voice:

> What, fear you not the fury of your king?

It is not in Edward but in Tamburlaine too, Marlowe has shown the magic power associated with a crown. To a straight question which is harsh and uncivil as put by Trussel to the king, "will you resign or not?", Edward's emphatic denial, "I'll not resign" is less a gesture of obduracy and more of reenergized confidence. Calling them traitors, he asks them to withdraw.

> Traitors, be gone, and join you with Mortimer!
> Elect, conspire, install, do what you will:
> Their blood and yours shall seal these treacheries![35]

And finally on Leicester's persuasions, Edward parts with the crown saying "What the heavens appoint I obey". He wishes to be oblivious of everything, including his own self. The lines are a fine penetrating study of a state of mind on verge of slipperiness of power from one's fingers.

> Here, here! (Gives the crown) Now, sweet God of heaven,
> Make me despise this transitory pomp,

And sit for aye enthronised in heaven!
Come, death, and with thy fingers close my eyes,
Or, if I live, let me forget my self![36]

He also gives a handkerchief wet with tears and dried with sighs for Isabel, expecting that its very sight will soften her heart and humanize the beast in her.

The Bishop of Winchester delivers the crown to Isabella and tells her that the king willingly resigned the crown which is a "happy news" for her. With the crown under the possession, the queen is not a simple woman in Elizabethan sense. The Bishop also informs her about the change of place of imprisonment and Kent's plot of "setting his brother free". Since the lord of Berkeley is described to be pitiful and generous as the Earl of Leicester was, Isabella instantly orders for a change in the guardian, thereby paving way for the entry of the two equally Machiavellian courtiers, Matrivis and Gurney who represent the characteristic image of a Renaissance courtier. Marlowe found all alike, high and low, being overpossessed by the mysterious tragic urge of the times.

Prince Edward is unwilling to wear the crown because he remains untouched by the power-quest and partly because he is alive to the Christian ideal of order and unity whereas Isabel is a case of moral distraction and, fearing that the Prince's conduct may frustrate the entire stratagem, she removes him from the scene and takes him to some other part of the palace. She tells a lie that it is "his highness pleasure". After Kent's abortive attempt fails to rescue the king Mortimer accuses him of disloyalty to the crown. Kent leaves the place with the bold promise to rescue the aged Edward from his foes but is beheaded.

Left alone with Mortimer, Isabella's mind freely wanders over the fanciful illusory materialistic pursuits which come with the power. It is the craziness of power that has destroyed her humanity to the degree that she loses sense of discrimination between the human and the non-human. Her interest is not nationalistic, nor does she show any patriotic sentiments. The only game she revels in is the power-game which, it is a pity, had corroded the finer sensibilities in her. The display of the bestial is seen in her suggestion of the king's murder in the guise of the safety of the Prince whereas the fact is that it is not the Prince but they (Mortimer and Isabella) themselves suffer from the persistent sense of insecurity and reversal of fortune. And if there is any threat to the life of the Prince it is from within, not without. The idea of the king's murder is a welcoming proposal for a power-seeker Mortimer. J.B. Steane observes that "She comes to depend on Mortimer and with him she degenerates. Weakness has become evil in her half ashamed admission, that she would welcome Edward's death."[37] The change in her conduct from a meek and humble woman to a confirmed dissembler is much criticized. Clifford Leach points out that "the change from the wronged but loving wife to the woman acquiescent in her husband's murder has commonly been regarded as a blemish on the play".[38] Following this line of criticism it is said that Isabella holds the destiny of the play which is not wholly true and if we accept this view then the Gaveston theme which is at the centre of the play is overshadowed. The truth is that she is a creature of the same class and times as Edward is. If Edward has the right to have his way, so does she have to go individualistic. And if both suffer it is so because they espouse a philosophy of laissez-faire in morals, a philosophical puzzle why, despite the Renaissance humanist's glorification of man, man has not been able to do away with evil.

Edward in captivity is treated as if he is a commoner. The barbaric cruelties heaped on him are characteristic of equally a barbaric conduct of the men in power. As per directions, the two conductors, Matrivis and Gurney, keep shifting the king from place to place, allowing him no rest. He is "vexed like a nightly bird/ Whose sight is loathsome to see winged birds". He feels restless with thirst and begs for water "to cool my thirst/ And clean my body from foul excrements". But they give him no water to drink and take him to a channel-water where he is washed and by force shaved lest he be recognized and rescued by his supporters. Edward invokes high powers to punish the wrong-doers which is ill-timed and misplaced. It is not that in Marlowe there is less intervention of the divine machinery, rather it is man who, as Faustus does, rejects God, not that God rejects man, and is thus deprived of self-esteem.

Immortal powers, that know the painful cares
That wait upon my poor distressed soul,
O, level all your looks upon these daring men
That wrong their liege and soverign, England's king.[39]

One of the maxims attributed to Machiavelli is that "it's better for a prince to be feared than loved". Mortimer is a case of distortion of Machiavellian precepts which are prescribed for a king to use in the interest of the state, not for an ambitious usurper. He knows that he is not a king, nor can he be one to ascend the throne. But it is he who is more alive to the power associated with the crown than other characters in the play. The fear in Machiavelli is evoked, partly by sense of reverence, shown to the king by the subjects, not by tyranny. His self-anointed image of a power-wielder is born of the imperfect understanding and ignorance of the moral laws governing monarchy. As Protector, the power to rule the realm becomes a shared venture between him and the queen. And since power corrupts, his cankerous mind gravitates toward evil. Satan overpowers Mortimer's heart and he immediately fixes his gaze on Edward's death.

The king must die, or Mortimer goes down.
The commons now begin to pity him:
Yet he that I the cause of Edward's death,
Is sure to pay for it when his son's of age;[40]

Like Satan he chooses evil 'to be my good'. But there God granted Satan's wish, in the world of men good or bad are worked out by what man does.

Marlowe brings into focus the sub-human conditions the king is subjected to in a dark dungeon of Berkeley Castle. The cruelties heaped on him are reported in words, not presented physically on the stage, partly for rousing the audience's sympathy and partly for theatrical limitations. This is made manifest in how the two custodians show their puzzlement over the sufferer's power of endurance.

MATREVIS: Gurney, I wonder the king dies not,
Being in a vault up the knees in water,
To which the channels of the castle run,
From whence a damp continually ariseth
That were enough to poison any man,
Much more a king, brought up so tenderly.
GURNEY: And so do I, Matrevis. Yesternight
I open'd but the door to throw him meat,
And I was almost stifled with the savour.
MATREVIS: He hath a body able to endure
More than we can inflict, and therefore now
Let us assail his mind another while.[41]

While Matrevis and Gurney are thinking of inventing new devices to assail the king's mind. Lightborn, a hired Italian murderer (he is outside history), drops in carrying the mysterious letter of Mortimer and becomes a point of focus. Lightborn is a professional murderer and can kill a man "bravely and be secret", his shadow falls on the king which is virtually the shadow of death. To the king's question "What light is that? Wherefore comes thou?" Lightborn's answer "To comfort you, and bring you joyful news" is intriguing. Edward sees little comfort in his looks, he calls him a villain saying "thou com'st to murder me". To it, Lightborn's reply is characteristic of his profession, ridden with irony.

To murder you, my most gracious lord?
Far is it from my heart to do you harm.
The queen sent me to see how you were us'd.
For she relents at this your misery:
And what eye can refrain from shedding tears.
To see a king in this most piteous state?[42]

Lightborn plays a dissembler. He expresses sorrow over the king's plight but the king sees in him the marching footsteps of death. He has the last jewel with which he proposes to seduce the killer. He expects that the killer perhaps would relent and be moved by his so pathetic a plight. He gives it to him which is symbolic of the separation of the last royal vestige, but it provokes no pity. The power of gold is paralysed!

A feathery bed is prepared for the king to rest and sleep. The dramatic tension increases with the ensuing silence. Edward lies on it fearing that it would be his last sleep and therefore all of a sudden he wakes to cry, "O, let me not die yet! Stay, O, stay a while!" On Lightborn's asking as to what makes him restless, Edward tells that he hears someone's voice buzzing in his ears warning him of death. In fact, there is none to call him, it is the hallucinatory impact of death-fright. Lightborn drops the 'cat and mouse play' and tells him in unambiguous words that he has come 'to rid thee of thy life'. At last finding no compassionate face nearby, Edward turns to God and invokes His mercy to receive his soul.

> I am too weak and feeble to resist,
> Assist me sweet God, and receive my soul.[43]

And as per directions, Matrevis lays the table on the apostate body of the king and stamps on it. A hot iron spit is thurst into his sides and with one heart-rending "wailful noyse" the king is murdered. The cease of the consistent beatings of the drum tells that the king is murdered. For a few seconds, the Berkeley Castle is darkened with horror: the death scene, Knox observes, "is difficult to match for the stark unrelieved pathos".[44] F.P. Wilson quotes Holinshed's words,[45] the details are "sordid, pitiless, horrible and Marlowe leaves out little". Charles Lamb observes that "the death scene of Marlowe's king moves pity and terror beyond any scene ancient or modern which I am acquainted...".[46] Clifford Leech's observation too is pertinent.

> The barbarity of these latter scenes makes them painful to read or to see or to speak of. No other tragic figure in Elizabethan or Jacobean times is treated in the degrading way that Mortimer permits for Edward. Henry VI is suddenly stabbed, Richard II dies fighting and eloquent, Richard III and Macbeth are killed in battle, the Duchess

> of Malfi makes a brave and pious speech before she is strangled, Marlowe's own Faustus dominates the scene in his hour of despair. The Jacobean playwrights could think of strange ways of torment and murder, but they never tear at our nerves as Marlowe does in this play.[47]

As per text of the letter what Gurney could understand is that he stabs Lightborn and throws his body into the moat to avoid suspicion. Matrevis comes to Mortimer carrying the king's dead body, the revelation of the murder is feared since Gurney has already disappeared to an obscure destination but Mortimer remains undismayed and unmoved. His Machiavellian advice to Matrevis "to fly to the savages" is a sure indication of the devilish designs to remove away the last conspirator from the scene. What a reward!

The word 'savages' is a powerful attestation of the fact that the act is barbaric and beastly. It partly brings out the 'savage' in Mortimer who has emerged triumphant in power-game by trapping an innocent queen into his lusty dreadful scheming. The imagery, he employs to define his own position in relation to other nobles, is highly suggestive for its implicit irony that hubris presages fall.

> As for myself, I stand as Jove's huge tree,
> And others are but shrubs compared to me,
> All tremble at my name, and I fear none,
> Let's see who dare impeach me for his death?[48]

The moral power governing the universe shows its hand. Edward's murder and the beastly alliance of the two criminals—Mortimer and Isabel—is revealed to the Prince (now king Edward III) through Mortimer's letter which Lightborn carried to the Castle. Mortimer is accused of treason and regicide and the Prince orders for his instant execution. The queen's mercy-appeal fails to save her lover who dies the terrible death of a traitor and she too is conveyed to the Tower which is outside history.

Mortimer is "Tamburlaine in a shrunken setting", he is as much a case of deluded self as the Scythian shepherd is. Both are destroyed by the false form of humanism and the resultant evils of unlimited passion for power. And because the stupendous vitality and the heroic Marlowe invests all his heroes with is misplaced, the venture is destined to final collapse. He makes his exit with the comment on the ever changing wheel of Fortune which is a sort of illumination, in Aristotelian sense, to learn the right relation between character and destiny.

> Base Fortune, now I see, that in thy wheel
> There is a point, to which when men aspire,
> They tumble headlong down: that point I touch'd,
> And, seeing there was no place to mount up higher,
> Why shall I grieve at my declining fall?
> Farewell, fair queen. Weep not for Mortimer,
> That scorns the world, and, as a traveler,
> Goes to discover countries yet unknown.[49]

The belief as enunciated by the theocentric humanism that the machinery governing the universe is divine, not diabolic, illumines the dark within the self. Mortimer knows that "there was no place to mount up higher" beyond a point he has touched which is a sort of realisation of man's place in the scheme of things. There is a division of power between man and God: Man can be a lord under the sky on the earth and beyond it is God's realm to rule. And therefore to go the Icarus way is destined to headlong fall. Mortimer makes a bid to exonerate himself from evil by passing the buck on to some one else. He calls fortune 'Base' simply because he cannot comprehend the philosophy, enshrined in the image of the revolving wheel, signifying in all its pervasiveness the doctrine of 'change' and 'continuity'. To accept its course is not simple stoicism "Why shall I grieve at my declining fall" that Baldock sounds "all live to die, and rise to fall". Mortimer's head is brought to king Edward III which must be a crude physical horror to the audience. He puts it on his father's hearse, pouring curses on it.

> Accursed head,
> Could I have rul'd thee then, as I do now,
> Thou hadst not hatch'd this monstrous treachery![50]

The fall of any prince is tragic but if it occurs through folly it hardly wins our imaginative sympathy. What strikes down Edward is the infatuation for the favourites as vanity and hideous rashness do Lear but he fails to rise to Lear's spiritual greatness. The Renaissance humanism recommends the "middle state" for the full flowering of the gifts God has given to man. Edward's tragedy issues from his failure to attain so. It is the perversion of normal human relationships that converts him into a voyeur who gloats over amorous 'shows' forbidden to human eye. The sin of ambition breeds hubris that enacts Mortimer's fall. The denial of life is manifest in Isabella too who succumbs to the Renaissance lust for power and leaves the stage with no longer a will to live, "Then come, sweet death and rid me of this grief"[51] which is contrary to the humanist spirit to be truly human.

NOTES

1. King Edward I banished Gaveston fearing his presence to be a demoralizing impact on the prince. And later when Edward ascended the throne he recalls him from the exile. Thus, he is virtually a bane of the king's ruination.
2. *Edward II*, ed. J.B. Steane, Penguin Classics, pp. 436-37.
3. Acateon, as the myth goes, was transformed into a stag and was devoured by his own dogs, his sin being the sin of passion to look at the goddess of hunting bathing naked, forgetting its moral hazards that what delights the senses may bring upon the onlooker the tragic doom.
4. *Edward II*, p. 439.
5. *Idem.*
6. *Idem.*
7. *Idem.*
8. *Ibid.*, p. 440.
9. *Idem.*
10. Phaeton was the son of Helios who borrowed the chariot from the sun for one day and drove it so dangerously close to the earth that Zeus struck him down to save the earth from catching fire. A chariot drive in Marlowe is the central image, be it upward, symbolizing man's aspirations or downward signifying his fall.

11. *Ibid.*, p. 449.
12. King Henry's tirade against the religious hegemony of the Roman church.

    Navarre, give me thy hand: I here do sear
    To ruinate that wicked Church of Rome,
    That hatcheth up such bloody practices;
    And here protest eternal love to thee,
    And to the Queen of England specially,
    Whom God hath bless'd for hating papistry.
    (*The Massacre of Paris*, pp. 582-83)
13. *Edward II*, p. 451.
14. *Ibid.*, p. 452.
15. *Ibid.*, p. 467.
16. *Ibid.*, p. 468.
17. *Ibid.*, p. 471.
18. *Idem.*
19. *Ibid.*, p. 472.
20. *Idem.*
21. *Ibid.*, p. 476.
22. *Ibid.*, p. 478.
23. *Ibid.*, p. 487.
24. *Idem.*
25. *Idem.*
26. *Ibid.*, p. 488.
27. *Ibid.*, p. 492.
28. *Ibid.*, p. 499.
29. *Idem.*
30. F.P. Wilson, "*Edward II*: Ironies of Kingship" in *Marlowe and the Early Shakespeare*, Oxford: Clarenden Press, 1953, p. 403.
31. *Edward II*, p. 508.
32. *Idem.*
33. Tisiphone is one of the three Furies in classical mythology with head covered with snakes instead of hair, signifying the eternal tormentation of the purgatory.

34. *Edward II*, p. 510.
35. *Idem.*
36. *Ibid.*, p. 511.
37. J.B. Steane, *Edward II*, *op. cit.*, p. 229.
38. Clifford Leech, "Marlowe's *Edward II*: Power and Suffering", *The Critical Quarterly*, Vol. I, No. 3, 1959, p. 190.
39. *Edward II*, p. 519.
40. *Ibid.*, p. 520.
41. *Ibid.*, p. 525.
42. *Ibid.*, p. 526.
43. *Ibid.*, p. 528.
44. Introduction to *Edward II*, ed. R.S. Knox; London: Methuen Educational Ltd., 1972, p. 22.
45. "The wail of the murdered man rang through the theatre as it did through the castle and town of Berkeley, so that divers being awakened therewith (as they themselves confessed) prayed heartily to God to receive his soul, when they understood by his cry what the matter meant" (in *Edward II: Ironies of Kingship*, p. 67).
46. Quoted in *Critics on Marlowe*, ed. Judith O' Neil, p. 15.
47. Clifford Leech, "*Edward II*: Power and Suffering", *op. cit.*
48. *Edward II*, p. 529.
49. *Ibid.*, p. 531.
50. *Ibid.*, p. 533.
51. *Idem.*

7

Conclusion

Thus, we come to an understanding that the humanism which Marlowe suggests to be a crying need for the next age to espouse is a new form of humanism which is based on "the middle path" between the Renaissance knowledge and medieval fatalism so that man, in a bid to be more than human, does not end less than human. His view of the universe is not wholly theocentric or anthropocentric because neither is wholly right or wrong. To take an extreme view of things, as they exist, leads to confusion and controversy.

The analyses of the foregoing chapters have convincingly demolished certain misconceptions about Marlowe's attitude to Christianity, even the accusations, and the vilifying campaign as unleashed against him by his fellow dramatists and Richard Baines' scandalous Note, are set aside by the critics as 'witch-hunt' and exaggeration. Frederick S. Boas' view is pertinent that "behind Marlower's exposure of the weakness of Christianity and Islam we seem to come closer than before to his own creed" which is akin to the humanism of the Greeks, known as the Christian humanism that flourished in the Middle Ages with the emphasis on the proposition that "one can be pro-man without being anti-God". Hence, the point is not of acceptance or rejection of the view whether the universe is man-centred or God-centred. What is of paramount interest is that any set of philosophical premises, in case they do not fit into the humanist programme, and take man away from the centre of Being, be discouraged. Marlowe's religious position in this regard is unambiguous and plain: when man can be rendered truly human by continuing to living with God, where is then the necessity to disown and seek separation from Him?

The new interpretation of the universe (that it is heliocentric) made man sceptic about the medieval truths, he no longer considered himself a sinner but a reservoir of unlimited potentialities. But does all this mean to be sceptical about the scriptural truths or seeking wilful divorce from God? The desire to know self in relation to God and universe is human but it loses its human appeal when it tends to overstep limitations and becomes untamed. The division in humanism as theocentric and anthropocentric humanism was an offshoot of man's deluded self, which, if it generated a heresy amounting to disowning God, it also brought the loss of self-esteem. Man, by virtue of his dual nature, flesh and spirit, is stationed in between with one foot upon the angelic ladder but his moving away from the centre to periphery brought a great upheaval in his original placement and what he lost during the process was, as Berdeyaev says, the spiritual centre of Being which involved the loss of his own self at the same time.

Keeping in view this newly-gained awareness which the Renaissance man developed, Marlowe invests his heroes with the extraordinary superhuman powers so as to enable them to stretch their imagination to the utmost bounds to realise their humanity and if at the end they are doomed, it is because of their wrong value orientation. They ignore the significance of the twin principles of humanism—freedom and responsibility—which can enable man to attain the Aristotelian idea of Magnificent Man, while walking between the 'new learning' and the medieval theology. The humanism which a Marlovian hero shares is a false form (anthropocentric) of humanism which, instead of creating the vision of heaven, takes him near to doleful shades of hell. But the phase is ephemeral, ultimately it is the spirit of true humanism which becomes triumphant. What does Faustus' cry for salvation in the last soliloquy or Edward's turning to God with the words in Act V, sc. vi—"Assist me, sweet God, and receive my soul!" —show? It sc. is sufficient to underline the truth that the heroic individualism, which they practice in absence of moral restraints, leads them nowhere.

Why did Marlowe choose to write tragedies, not comedies to project his view of man? Tragedy entails value and shows men nobler and heroic. But what value a Marlovian hero evolves and what nobility and heroic he puts forth for others to envy is a point of interest. Instead, what he does destroys the heroic in man which is a case of tragic waste and which urges upon the serious readers to reflect on as to where lies the wrong. Is Tamburlaine's mass slaughter, including Calyphas, his eldest son and the virgins of the Damascus, Barabas' wholesale destruction of the Christians and the non-Christians, including Abigail, his daughter, Edward's neglect of a virtuous queen and putting Warwick, Lancaster and the gentle Pembroke to death in retaliation nobler? Can this naked barbaric demonstration of human depravity render man truly human? No, certainly not. As a matter of truth what was condemned as vice in the Renaissance humanism was worshipped as virtue by Marlowe's heroes as Harry Levin says that his heroes "make their fortunes by exercising virtues which conventional morality will regard as vices".

In Marlowe-criticism there has also been much critical wrangling regarding what goes as Marlovian Trinity—Atheism, Epicureanism, Machiavellianism and the print of the dramatist's personality on his heroes. The critics labouriously relate his heroes' attitude to religion, with Marlowe's "unremitting warfare with Christianity" and in this context hold him "an atheist and a godlesse personne". But can one lose sight of the fact as to what is at the back of the image of man Marlowe projects in his plays in the age of modern scepticism and science? The gains of humanism lie in man's discovery of self and the universe, the full implications of which are that they are to render man truly human. And if Marlowe shows man becoming otherwise, is it heretical? Even the standard critics find the 'divinity of Christ no longer in question' in his plays. *Tamburlaine* is dismissed as anti-Christian play, simply because it nihilates the Christian virtues, like mercy, forgiveness, humility which is seen in the massacre of the innocent virgins of Damascus who come to seek Tambulaine's mercy. The truth is that man in a bid to defy what nature denies put those benefits to disuse and suffered damnation. The popular fallacy that Marlowe is nothing, if not personal seems to hold no water, he is, one can say, as much in Faustus as Shakespeare is in Hamlet. The total transcendence of individuality is hard to attain. Marlowe is "involved in the intellectual and spiritual revolution of the time" as M.M. Mahood observes but the treatment is not subjective. David Bevington and Rasmussen have also pointed out that Marlowe's plays cannot be straightway interpreted as autobiography. His sympathies could be with the characters in their seeking fulfillment to the utmost degree but he parts company when they, in a bid to be more than human, act as 'overreacher' and lose self-esteem. If Marlowe had supported their world outlook he would not have shown Barabas' overthrow in a boiling cauldron, or Faustus's passage to hell. Sartre's view of man that man is a 'project' is wholly true to Marlowe's heroes. The reward or punishment at the end are the fruits of the seeds sown.

Tamburlaine's notion of self-sufficiency generates in him the fond illusion that he can hold "the Fates bound fast in iron chains" which is a form of false humanism and which shatters at the end in the acquiescence of nature. The words he dies with, "For Tamburlaine, the Scourge of God must die" bring out the illusoriness of the dream of omnipotence and man's failure to come to terms with nature. This sense of waste and futility also haunts Faustus. He takes an Orphean plunge headlong into new forbidden areas of human experience and what remains of paramount interest to see is: where does this venture of the mind land him to? The problem is, therefore, epistemological: it is man's imperfect 'knowing' of the self and the resultant miscalculations that drives him toward destruction. Knowing that the world is unknowable and cannot be cognized as the idealists say, he feels irritated at mortal limitations and chooses to cognize it through magic, the failure of which is reflected in the end in the rejection of what he himself chooses. He talks of burning those necromantic books which once looked 'heavenly'. Hence, in place of moral progression and spiritual sufficiency there is regression and spiritual defeat.

Barabas's address to his own self in the boiling cauldron. "Then, Barabas, breathe forth thy latest fate", is significant. The words 'Thy latest fate' are the words of the dramatist which concern less with the fate of one Barabas but with that of all the worshippers of sham gods. This becomes all the more conspicuous when we see even the characters of lesser significance falling prey to the lust for power, gold and pleasure. The struggle of the two holy friars, Bernardine and Jacomo to convert Barabas into their respective order and possess his gold is symbolic of the capitalist's struggle against each other in a bourgeois society. The trio 'Bellamira-Pilia Borja-Ithamore' are too destroyed by the magic power of gold. Gaveston, the king's 'minion' mounts high on the borrowed waxen-wings and does not hesitate to assault the clergy and the nobility. He calls the barons "Base, leaden earls". In derision, he asks them to go home and come not near "to scoff at Gaveston/ Whose mounting thoughts did never creep so low/ As to bestow a look on such as you." It is the overdose of royal patronage and hubris that turns him into an 'overreacher'. He is beheaded for this act of moral effrontery under the surfeit of power and pleasure.

Marlowe is thus the first analyst of the moral decay set in the Renaissance. His diagnosis of this moral malaise and the anatomy of nature in its inevitability of striving after power and pleasure is prophetic in the sense that, if the striving tends to be erring and individualistic, it leads to frustrating the very notion of humanism. Marlowe's departure from the Athenian tragedy in certain matters further underlines his philosophy of life and art. The point is not as to how much he owes to Aristotle in regard to projecting the tragic dilemma of his age on the stage, but how he looked upon the contemporary scene in the 16th century England from the viewpoint of a tragic artist and how it finds reflection in his plays. He is a realist who has shown in his plays what man is and how he acts and reacts in a given situation. A situation is created which, by nature, is what human heart aspires for but which is also a test of his humanity, hard for him to surmount. Marlowe takes cognizance both of man's strength and weaknesses. If he shows the heroic in man to the utmost degree, he, at the same time, shows him, in weaker moments, succumbing to passion which destroys his humanity and brings ruination.

Since his theatre is a projection of the early phase of Renaissance which is characterized by optimism, romantic exuberance and untrammelled individualism, there is little struggle at the level of the characters to fight evil within and in the outer world as Hamlet does for a moral purge in Denmark. However, Abigail in *The Jew of Malta* and Prince Edward (*Edward II*) are his positive creations of true humanism who struggle against disvalues and injustice, being done to them: one dies of poison which is a case of tragic waste, the other ascends to the throne which signifies the ultimate victory of moral sense over the forces of chaos and disorder.

Bibliography

Primary Sources

Christopher Marlowe: The Complete Plays, ed. by J.B. Steane, Penguin Books, 1969.

——. *Tamburlaine, Part One.*

——. *Tamburlaine, Part Two.*

——. *Doctor Faustus.*

——. *The Jew of Malta.*

——. *Edward, the Second.*

Secondary Sources: Books/Journals

Ahmad, S. Mustaq. *Existential Aesthetics: A Study of Jean Paul Sartre's Theory of Art and Literature*, New Delhi: Atlantic Publishers, 1991.

Bakeless, John. *Christopher Marlowe*, Cape, 1938.

Bernard, Robert. *A Short History of English Literature.* (Second edition), Oxford: Blackwell, 1994.

Bevington, David and Eric Rasmussen (ed.). *Marlowe: Tamburlaine Part I, Part II, Doctor Faustus, The Jew of Malta, Edward II in the World's Classics Series*, Oxford Uni. Press, 1995.

Blackham, H.J. *Six Existential Thinkers*, London, 1985.

Bradbrook. M.C. "A Discussion of *Tamburlaine*" in *Themes and Conventions of Elizabethan Tragedy*. Cambridge: Cambridge Uni. Press, 1935.

Boas, Fredreick S. *Christopher Marlowe: A Biographical and Critical Study*. Oxford: The Clerenden Press, 1940.

——. (ed.) *The Tragical History of Doctor Faustus*, London: Methuen and Co. Ltd., 1932.

Brinton, Crane. *The Shaping of the Modern Mind*, New York: Mentor Books, 1953.

Bouwsma, William, J. *The Interpretation of Renaissance Humanism*, Washington: Service Centre of Teachers of History, 1959.

Brooke, Nicholas. "The Moral Tragedy of *Doctor Faustus*" in *The Cambridge Journal*, Vol. V, No. 11, 1952, pp. 666-87.

Burckhardt, Jacob. *The Civilisation of the Renaissance in Italy*, Oxford, London: Phaidon Press, 1945.

Bush, Douglas. *Prefaces to Renaissance Literature*, New York: W.W. Norton and Company Inc., 1965.

——. *The Renaissance and English Humanism*, Toronto: University of Toronto Press, 1962.

Camus, Albert. *The Rebel*, trans. by Authony Bower, London: Penguin Books Ltd., 1975.

Campana, A. "The Origin of the Word Humanism" in *The Journal of the Warburg and Courtauld Institutes*, IX, 1946, pp. 60-75.

Charlton, H.B. and R.D. Waller (eds.). *Edward II*, London: Methuen and Co. Ltd., 1955.

Chandra, Naresh. *The Literature of the English Renaissance*, Delhi: Doaba House, 1985.

Cole, Douglas. *Suffering and Evil in the Plays of Christopher Marlowe*, rept., New York: Gordian Press, 1972.

Eliot, T.S. *Elizabethan Dramatists*, London: Faber and Faber, 1968.

——. "The Duchess of Malfi", *The Listener*, XXXVI, 18 December, 1941, pp. 825-26.

Ferguson, Wallace K. *The Renaissance in Historical Thought: Five Centuries of Interpretation*, Boston: Houghton Miffin, 1948.

Una Ellis, Fermor (ed.). *Tamburlaine the Great in Two Parts*, London: Methuen and Co. Ltd., 1930.

Greg. W.W. "The Damnation of Faustus" in Clifford Leech (ed.). *Marlowe: A Collection of Critical Essays*, Prentice Hall, Inc., 1964.

Gardner, Helen. "The Second Part of Tamburlaine the Great" in *Modern Language Review*, Vol. XXXVII, 1942, pp. 18-24.

Henderson, Philip. *Christopher Marlowe*, Longmans, Green, 1952.

Irvine, Hellen Douglas, W.D. Macinnes. *A History of English Literature*, Vol. I, Delhi: Royal Publications, 1992.

Jack, Ian. "The Case of John Webster", *Scrutiny*, XVI, 1949, pp. 38-43.

Jaspers, Karl. *Existentialism and Humanism*, trans. by E.B. Asthor, New York, 1952.

Kaufmann, W. *Existentialism from Dostoevsky to Sartre*, New York: 1956.

Knights, L.C. "The Strange Case of Christopher Marlowe" in *Further Explorations*. Chatto and Windus, 1965.

Krischbaum, Leo. "Marlowe's Faustus: A Reconsideration" in *Review of English Studies*, XIX, 1943, pp. 225-41.

Kristeller, Paul Oskar. *Renaissance Thought II: Papers on Humanism and the Arts*, New York: Harper and Row Publishers, 1965.

——. *Renaissance Thought: The Classic Scholastics, and Humanist Strains*, New York: Harper and Row Publishers, 1961.

Kocher, Paul H. *Christopher Marlowe: A Study of His Thoughts, Learning and Character*, University of North Carolina Press, 1946.

Leech, Clifford. "Edward II: Power and Suffering" in *Critical Quarterly*, Vol. 1, No. 3, 1959.

——. "The Structure of Tamburlaine" in *Tulane Drama Review*, 8, No. 4, 1964, pp. 32-46.

Levin, Harry. *Christopher Marlowe: The Overreacher*, London: Faber and Faber Ltd., 1954.

Long, Williams J. *English Literature: Its History and Its Significance*. Ludhiana: Kalyani Publishers, 1989.

Lukacs, Georg. *Goethe and His Age* (translated by Robert Anchor), London: Marlin Press, 1968.

Maxwell, J.C. "The Plays of Christopher Marlowe" in *The Pelican Guide to English Literature*, ed. Boris Ford, Vol. II, Penguin Books, 1954-61.

Machiavelli, Niccolo. *The Prince*, trans, by George Bull, Penguin Books Ltd., 1977.

Mahood, M.M. "The Jew of Malta: A Contracted World", from 'Marlowe's Heroes' in *Poetry and Humanism*, Cape, 1950.

——. *Poetry and Humanism*, London, The Camelot Press Ltd., 1950.

Niebuhr, R. *The Nature and Destiny of Man—I*, New York, 1941.

Orestein, Robert. *The Moral Vision of Jacobean Tragedy*, Madison, 1960.

Peet, Donald. "The Rhetoric of *Tamburlaine*" in *ELH*, 26, 1959, pp. 137-55.

Plumb, J.H. *The Penguin Books of the Renaissance*, Harmondsworth, Middlesex, England: Penguin Books Ltd., 1964.

Poirier, Michel. *Christopher Marlowe*. Chatto and Windus, 1951.

Quinn, Michael. "The Freedom of Tamburlaine", *Modern Language Quarterly*, 21, 1960, pp. 315-20.

Rabakin, Norman. *Reinterpretation of Elizabethan Drama*, New York, London: Columbia University Press, 1969.

Ribner, Irving (ed.). *Christopher's Tamburlaine Fart One and Part Two: Text and Major Criticism*. Indianapolis: The Odyssey Press, 1974.

——. "Marlowe and Machiavelli", in *Comparative Literature*, 6, 1954, pp. 348-56.

——. *The English History Plays in the Age of Shakespeare*, Princeton: Princeton Univ. Press, 1957.

Richard, Susan. "Marlowe's *Tamburlaine* II, A Drama of Death" in *Modern Language Quarterly*, 26, 1965, pp. 375-87.

Rickett, Arthur Compton. *A History of English Literature*, New Delhi: UBS Publishers Ltd., 1997.

Rossister, A.P. *English Drama From Early to the Elizabethans*, 1950, pp. 157-59.

Sartre, J.P. *Being and Nothingness*, trans. by Hazel E. Barnes, New York: Gramerey Books, 1956.

——. *Existentialism and Humanism*, trans. by Philip Mariet, London, 1948.

Smith, Warren D. "The Substance of Meaning in *Tamburlaine* Part I" in *Studies in Philology*, 67, 1970, pp. 156-66.

Spence, Leslie. "*Tamburlaine* and Marlowe" in *PMLA*, 42, 1927, pp. 604-22.

Steane, J.B. *Marlowe: A Critical Study*, London: Cambridge University Press, 1964.

Waith, Eugene. "Edward II: The Shadow of Action", *Tulane Drama Review*, 8; 4, Summer, 1964.

Weiss, R. *Humanism in England during the Fifteenth Century*, Oxford, 1941.

Williams, Raymond. *Modern Tragedy*, London: The Hogarth Press, 1992.

Wilson, F.P. "Edward II, Ironies of Kingship" in *Marlowe and the Early Shakespeare*. Oxford: The Clareden Press, 19563, pp. 90-103.

Index